THE NEW YORK TIMES

BOOK OF
VEGETABLE
GARDENING

by Joan Lee Faust

color illustrations by Allianora Rosse

Quadrangle/*The New York Times Book Co.*

THE NEW YORK TIMES

BOOK OF VEGETABLE GARDENING

PHOTO CREDITS

Ray Almquist, p. 10
Herman Gantner, pp. 6 (top), 25, 27, 40, 57, 61, 66, 69, 72, 204 (top), 209, 218, 225
The New York Times/Bill Aller, p. 252 (bottom)
The New York Times/George Tames, p. 252 (top)
George Taloumis, pp. 4, 6 (bottom), 13, 204 (bottom), 212
Mason Weymouth, p. 254

Library of Congress Cataloging in Publication Data

Faust, Joan Lee.
 The New York Times book of vegetable gardening.

 Bibliography: p.
 Includes index.
 1. Vegetable gardening. I. Title.
SB321.F275 1975   635   74-80483
ISBN 0-8129-0501-6

Second printing, May 1975

BOOK DESIGN: BETTY BINNS
LINE DRAWINGS: GRAMBS MILLER

contents

planning
and
planting

why grow your own?

Some vegetable seeds are very small. Something happens to gardeners when they see these minute expressions of life, sown so carefully, breaking ground. In no time at all tiny plants become full-sized lettuces, beets, carrots, and onions. An enthusiastic family shares them at the dinner table and finds the freshness of the flavors beyond description, worth every minute of the time and care that produced them.

Though planting and harvesting have gone on since time immemorial and there is nothing new in the routine, rare is the person who does not feel a sense of wonderment. A warmth glows inside, an appreciation, an affection, a love for nature's world and all that it brings forth. Vegetable growing yields not only a generous harvest, but deep satisfaction, happiness, and other intangible rewards.

These inner responses are no doubt one of the reasons why there is a boom in vegetable gardening, but there are other reasons as well. A poll taken by the famous Gallup organization attributes it to a new way of life, a revolution back to the land. Their survey has shown a marked increase in vegetable gardening in recent years; nearly four out of ten households now keep a vegetable plot. As many as one-fourth of the public surveyed indicated they would like to attend classes on vegetable raising, and those without vegetable gardens would like to have them.

3 Whether or not the boom continues, according to the

Gallup poll, depends on the five Es—energy, economy, ecology, exercise, and extra time. Energy restrictions are encouraging more back-yard vacations and less free-wheeling travel. A leaning toward gardening as a means of recreation follows. Economics—the high totals rung up at the supermarket check-out counter—is resulting in a real necessity for families to grow their own.

Statistics on how much is actually saved by growing your own show wide variations, as costs of materials and market values of produce vary. However, when the time spent is regarded as recreational and man-hours are not calculated, the savings can be considerable. Estimates show that a family of four can save between $200 and $300 annually and more when produce is stored, canned, or frozen. The dawning of the four-day work week, allowing more leisure time, may naturally spur more home "market gardening."

What are the most popular vegetables grown in the United States? According to surveys of leading seedsmen, they are tomatoes, beans, corn, cucumbers, peas, lettuce, radishes, squash, melons, and beets. Peppers would also be high on the list if the survey had included transplant sales at garden centers.

The most popular vegetables are actually the ten that are easiest to raise, and are excellent choices for those launching their first vegetable garden. As confidence grows, the more difficult crops can be mastered, especially the cabbage family—broccoli, cabbage, kale, and Brussels sprouts.

Beginning gardeners often make the same mistakes—growing too much and making the garden too big. Be warned! Start small, and let the vegetable garden grow with the family's appetite and your own know-how.

Grow what the family likes to eat. The garden center seed rack is a little like a buffet table, but no gardener is obligated to try a little bit of everything. Have a family powwow first, decide what vegetables the family will eat, and plan to grow them, saving a nook or two for a few oddities or specialties. And don't forget that since many crops, such as radishes, lettuce, beets, beans, carrots, and onions, will mature before the summer is over, your garden design should include succession plantings to keep the garden space continually productive, or weeds will take over. And to be sure that the bean, corn, radish, or carrot crops don't come all at once, plant only portions

The thrill of harvest from cucumbers and beets is but part of the reward.

of the rows at 2-week intervals to keep the harvest maturing gradually.

There is no need to make the vegetable garden a traditional, squared-off, 10 × 12- or 15 × 20-foot plot. Vegetables grow well with flowers, and many a fine vegetable harvest can be achieved with lettuce edging a flower border, eggplants and peppers alternating with zinnias, tubs of tomatoes, peppers, cucumbers, and eggplant lining a patio. Window boxes that receive plenty of sun are marvelous places for salad crops, herbs, and even cherry tomatoes. Windowsill pots will support a harvest of parsley, radishes, leaf lettuce, chives, and even dill. Vegetable gardening can truly be for everyone who has inventiveness, imagination, and spunk. Never say no—it can be done.

Vegetables need a place in the sun where the soil drains easily.

7

getting
started

Vegetables are sun lovers, and require at least six hours of sunlight a day. Ideally, the sky should be clear overhead all day long, from sunup to sundown. This means the garden must be planted well away from the shade of trees or buildings. If the only site is one that is sunny in the morning and again late in the afternoon, then the vegetables will have to grow there—but results will not be tops. The key to a bountiful vegetable harvest is continuous, fast growth, which depends on a sunny site with good soil.

Be wary of tree roots, too. They usually extend quite far from the trunk, at least as far as the outer branches. Roots will compete with the vegetables for soil nutrients, and the vegetables will usually lose out.

Few if any vegetables will grow in the shade. Salad greens—lettuce, endive, spinach, corn salad, rugola— may do fairly well, since leaves are what the plant must produce for harvest. But a vegetable that must develop roots—carrots, beets, radishes, turnips—or fruit—tomatoes, peppers, eggplant, squash—needs sun.

Conditions on even a relatively small area will differ. In the early spring, walk around your back yard or property to see where the snow melts first, where the sun catches in warm pockets. In the colder climes, paying attention to these small microclimates will make a difference in how vegetables respond during the growing season. Be wary of low areas, where water tends to stand in puddles after rains.

The second need for good growth is loamy, well-drained soil. Few garden sites have the ideal soil, but proper soil management can turn even the most poorly drained clay soils into a fertile loam in a few years. (More on this in the chapter on soil.)

A flat garden is obviously much easier to tend than one on a slope. But if a slope it must be, hopefully the hill side slopes gradually, not more than 3 or 4 percent. Run the rows across, not up and down, to discourage soil erosion and catch as much rain as possible. A good mulch system will help catch water and control erosion. For a steep slope, terracing with stones or railroad ties will be necessary.

Third, the vegetable plot should be near a water supply. Although it may seem hard to believe, most vegetables are about 90 percent water. This makes soil moisture essential if the crop is to develop quickly. A heavy mulch will reduce the need for water, but in general at least 1 inch of water a week, either through natural rainfall or irrigation, is required. A long hose may be one of your most important investments, especially in hot climates.

A fourth consideration is for those who live on large acreages or in rural areas. Keep the garden as near the house as possible for several reasons. First, it is easy to tend, and only a short walk to bring in the harvest. If the garden is near the house, much greater use will be made of it for salad lunches, herb flavoring, or last-minute dinner ideas when the cook runs out of inspiration. And a vegetable garden near a house will tend to discourage nature's raiders—rabbits, raccoons, deer, mice, and opossums. A fence is the best deterrent and may be required.

catalog homework

Since a vegetable gardener starts with seeds, the more he knows what is available, the better he can choose and plan. In addition to reading this book, some additional homework will be required, but work that most find engrossing and delightful—catalog study. The addresses of the major seedsmen who publish mail-order catalogs are listed on page 276. Most of them are free, ordered with a simple postal card; a few cost a nominal sum.

Some seedsmen sell exclusively through catalogs. Some

*Choosing the right
seed packet is such
a puzzlement.*

sell exclusively through seed racks at garden centers, supermarkets, dime stores, and so forth.

The advantages of ordering through catalogs are two-fold: first come, first served. When only limited quantities of particular varieties are available, mail orders are filled first. Thus mail-order gardeners will have the specific seed varieties they want to grow when they want to plant them. Second, many catalogs feature garden supplies as well as seeds. Spring shopping can be done with one filled-in order blank and a personal check sent in the mail.

Catalogs start arriving soon after the Christmas mail rush is over, and seed packets start appearing in garden center racks in late winter. If an order was placed with a seed company the previous year, the new seed catalog will come automatically. You may have to write for a new catalog each year if no orders have been placed.

Each catalog carries a broad range of vegetable selections that would fill almost every gardener's needs. But not every vegetable is listed in every catalog, so it is more practical to have several. Besides, they are fun to read, especially when outdoor winter snows and winds are blustering about.

The first pages of the seedsmen's book usually display, in tempting, full-color photos, the new introductions for the year. These are worth looking into, because seedsmen are ever trying to better their offerings to improve harvests and customer satisfaction. The back page usually is where you will find all the particulars about ordering, postal costs, and so forth. In between are the wonderful nitty-gritty facts about the vegetables (and flowers). The vegetables grouped alphabetically, have several pages devoted to each and include the many named varieties sold. Each variety named will be followed by a notation, such as "21 days," "40 days," or "90 days." This notation is very important, for it is the field-tested estimate as to how many days are required from outdoor planting time to harvest. For transplants, 3 to 4 weeks can be lopped off the total, for the seed is given a head start indoors. However, don't hold the seedsmen to these figures exactly. Much depends on the weather and soil variations. But the figure is fairly accurate, and essential for planning.

When reading a catalog, keep a pencil handy to jot down those vegetables that are potentials; at least underline them, or make some other kind of notation. And read all the catalogs first before settling on choices. Finally, and this is very important, check your choices against the recommended lists (included in the vegetable section; some seedsmen may star, print in bold face, or bull's-eye those varieties they feel are of special merit for flavor and quality), as well as lists supplied by your local office of Cooperative Extension in cooperation with the state's agricultural school. These selected varieties are chosen for best flavor and yield. Some varieties are bred particularly for chosen geographical areas, and it makes good sense to follow these leads.

One of the best ways to eliminate disease problems in a vegetable garden is to grow the disease-resistant varieties. Some seeds are pretreated with fungicides to ward off germination problems caused by soil fungi. There are many available, and the catalog copy will make note of any bred-in resistance.

The words "hybrid" or "F_1 hybrid" will also be included in many vegetable descriptions. A hybrid is a cross between two parents, each with superior qualities combining in a superior offspring. The offspring (hybrid) will be better than either parent. Most hybrids are sterile, and their seed should not be saved.

An F_1 hybrid is a superduper hybrid, bred from carefully selected inbred lines. The lines are established for particular qualities, such as disease resistance, earliness, flavor, stamina, color. The offspring, or F_1 hybrids, of these inbred lines are marked by uniformity in their appearance and qualities. Because they are usually hand pollinated rather than open-field pollinated, the seed is more expensive. In the garden the vegetables will usually be sterile and will not seed.

Here are a few other notations to be alert to when reading seed catalogs. Special collection offers at reduced rates are handy money savers for those with small gardens or those who do not have time to think out and plan their own plots. The seedsmen have already done it, and with a price saving offer as well.

A few varieties will be marked "AAS." This designates that the particular variety won an All-American Selections Award. This nonprofit testing system, established by the seedsmen, examines new vegetable introductions in field trials throughout the country. If they prove to be superior to existing varieties, they receive a nomination for an AAS award. They are reliable, with excellent quality and taste.

Well-staked and pruned tomato plants will produce a bountiful crop.

12

And last, seedsmen often like to include some odd and interesting vegetables, which they call "novelties." These are offbeat vegetables, odd varieties that may grow dwarf or tall. They are fun to try. But for the main part of the vegetable garden, rely on the tried and true.

If the first year you are thoroughly bewildered by the choices of what to grow, here is a tip. Try the "perishables" first—the vegetables that do not ship readily. The big five are corn, peas, tomatoes, beans, and leaf lettuce. And for anyone who feels particularly adventurous at the start, add asparagus and broccoli.

how much?

If you want to plant more than the big five, be practical. Seed catalogs are so enticing you may find yourself with a list of seeds requiring a garden far larger than you are able to handle.

How much to order? Usually, one seed packet is sufficient for the average home garden (see chart page 20). But keep in mind two things. Where crops are to be resown in midsummer, plan on a second packet. For some crops, like beans and peas, it may be more practical to buy ¼ pound or ½ pound quantities, depending on the family's appetite. These crops also freeze well. Be sure to order enough seed for the whole summer, since by early June stocks are often depleted, and the seed racks in supermarkets and garden centers are stripped. Dealers usually take back any leftover stocks in July.

When making out your seed order, list separately the seed that will be sown outdoors directly, then list the seed that will be started indoors and transplanted outdoors later. Many gardeners prefer to buy transplants from garden centers and forgo the challenge of starting seed indoors.

putting it all together

Several garden plans are shown on pages 15–18 to guide the putting together of the family vegetable plot. As noted earlier, vegetables do not always have to be planted in an exclusive squared-off area; they can be tucked in flower borders, along shrubbery foundations, or in window boxes, or trained along fences. Be imaginative, and utilize every bit of garden space practically and

14

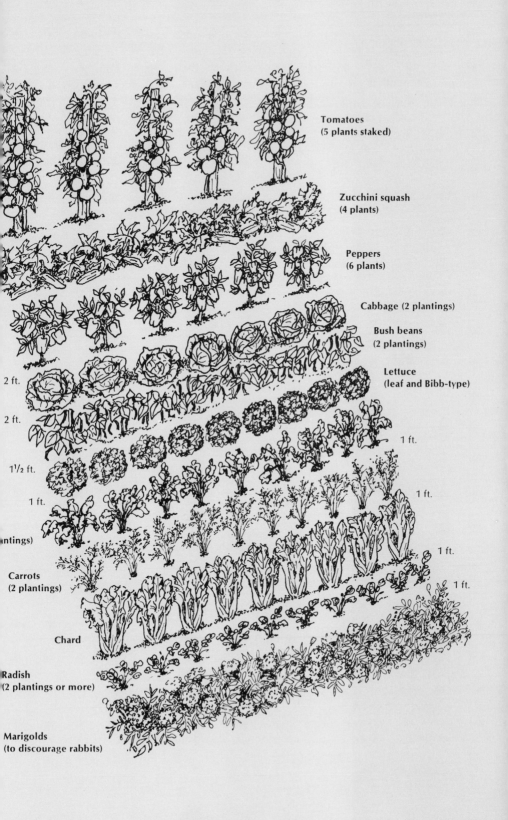

Tomatoes
(5 plants staked)

Zucchini squash
(4 plants)

Peppers
(6 plants)

Cabbage (2 plantings)

Bush beans
(2 plantings)

Lettuce
(leaf and Bibb-type)

2 ft.

2 ft.

1½ ft.

1 ft.

1 ft.

1 ft.

1 ft.

1 ft.

ntings)

Carrots
(2 plantings)

Chard

Radish
(2 plantings or more)

Marigolds
(to discourage rabbits)

Family vegetable garden

This 12 x 25 foot vegetable garden designed by the National Garden Bureau features 18 varieties of vegetables to feed a family of four with plenty left over for canning and freezing.

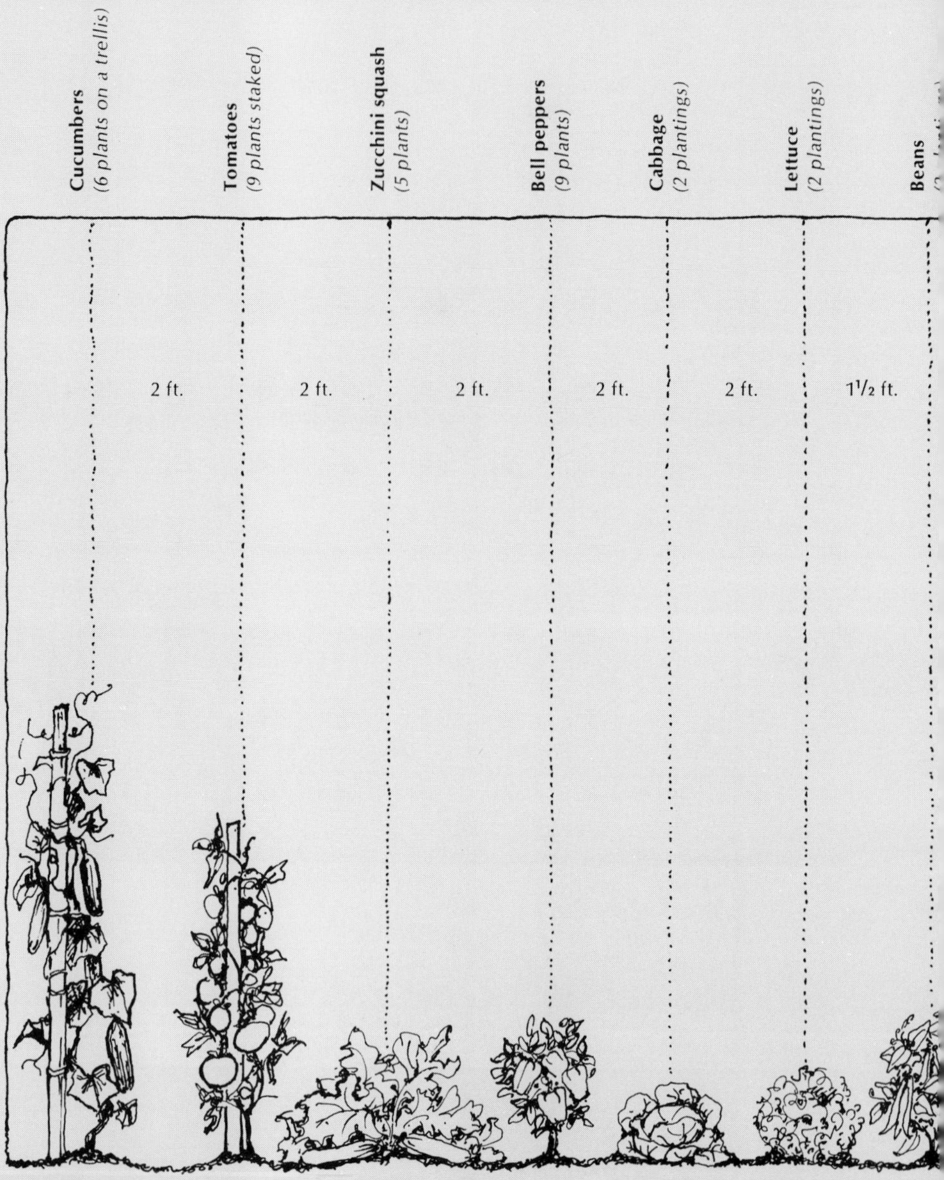

Cucumbers
(6 plants on a trellis)

Tomatoes
(9 plants staked)

Zucchini squash
(5 plants)

Bell peppers
(9 plants)

Cabbage
(2 plantings)

Lettuce
(2 plantings)

Beans

2 ft.   2 ft.   2 ft.   2 ft.   2 ft.   1½ ft.

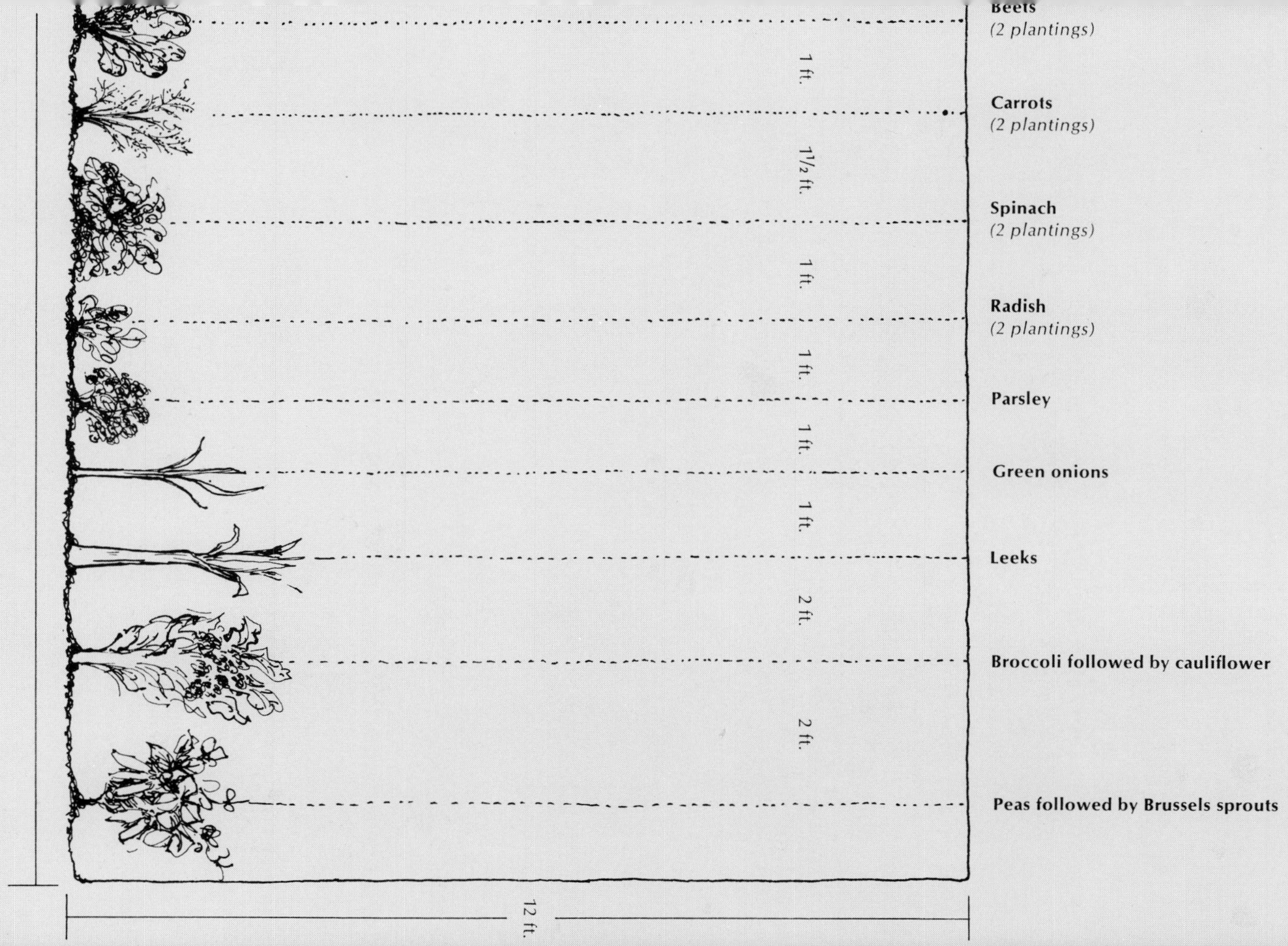

Beets
(2 plantings)

Carrots
(2 plantings)

Spinach
(2 plantings)

Radish
(2 plantings)

Parsley

Green onions

Leeks

Broccoli followed by cauliflower

Peas followed by Brussels sprouts

1 ft. 1½ ft. 1 ft. 1 ft. 1 ft. 1 ft. 2 ft. 2 ft.

12 ft.

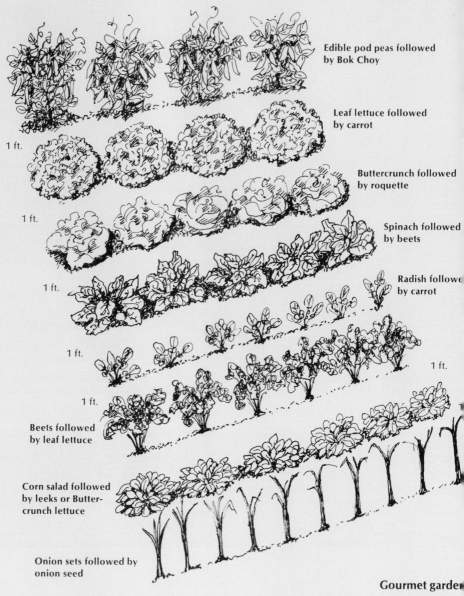

Edible pod peas followed
by Bok Choy

Leaf lettuce followed
by carrot

1 ft.

Buttercrunch followed
by roquette

1 ft.

Spinach followed
by beets

1 ft.

Radish followe
by carrot

1 ft.

1 ft.

1 ft.

Beets followed
by leaf lettuce

Corn salad followed
by leeks or Butter-
crunch lettuce

Onion sets followed by
onion seed

Gourmet garde

*A tiny 4 x 8 easy-to-care-for garden t
grow unusual salads and vegetable
where space is limited. Ideal for retiree
or condominium residents. Three tub
are also suggested to grow cherr
tomatoes, garden cress, and basil on
sunny patio*

pleasingly. And don't overlook the mini or dwarf vegetables especially suited for small spaces (see Vegetables to Grow Section).

The garden plans show how far apart rows should be spaced, as does the color section, Vegetables to Grow. Details on planting are given there, too. Most of the root crops and leafy crops can be planted fairly close together, 12 to 18 inches apart, allowing enough space for cultivating, weeding, and picking. The big space takers are corn, melons, squash, tomatoes, and cucumbers. However, some vegetables, such as pole beans, cucumbers, and squash can be trained on fences, trellises, or poles. If grown on a fence or trained on a trellis, cucumbers need only 2½ feet of row space.

Graph paper is very handy for laying out a vegetable garden. Mark each row on the paper and allow the proper spacing. Check the days to maturity in the seed catalog and plan for second crops where short-season crops such as beans, beets, and radishes will vacate the rows before the growing season is half over. Plan to sow portions of the rows where long-season harvest will be needed, and mark exactly where each transplant will go to allow the proper spacing.

Watch how the sun travels across the garden and line out the rows so they run north and south for fullest exposure to the sun. Also keep the taller crops—corn and tomatoes—to the back or one side of the garden, and graduate down to the shorter crops—beans, spinach, beets, and salad greens.

If the ground is sloping, run the rows across. Jot down on the plan, in pencil, the planting dates expected. Then write in ink what day the seed or plants are actually set out. This will be a good reference for the following year.

Each year variations and changes should be made in plans to keep the soil productive and to keep you from falling into a rut.

Since the neophyte does have a tendency to plant too much, it is better to start small and expand as the years progress, or as the family grows in size. For example, one tomato plant per person is sufficient, with an extra or two added for sharing with neighbors. Obviously, if there are plans to can tomatoes for the winter season, one per person is not enough. But neither is it practical to plant two dozen plants for a family of four unless they thrive on tomatoes morning, noon, and night.

A short row, 3 feet long, of summer squash will keep a family of four in squash very nicely. Two hills of cucumbers will provide all they can eat.

As a guide to planning, the following lists will help decide space allotments. Plan to keep the garden rows filled and productive throughout the entire growing season.

Sow or plant in cool weather

Beets/chard	Onions	Spinach
Cabbage/broccoli,	Parsley	Turnips
Brussels sprouts	Peas	
Lettuce	Radishes	

Sow or plant in warm weather

Beans	Eggplant	Melons
Carrots	Peppers	Okra
Corn	Squash	
Cucumbers	Tomatoes	

One crop a season (space taker-uppers and slow growers)

Corn	Peppers	New Zealand spinach
Eggplant	Tomatoes	Potatoes
Melons	Summer squash	
Leeks	Winter squash	

Resowers (more than one crop a season)

Beans	Kohlrabi	Spinach
Beets	Lettuce	Turnips
Carrots	Radishes	
Cabbage family	Rutabagas	

soil

Good soil management is the key that opens the lock to successful vegetable gardens. No matter how poor the soil may be at the start, proper management will gradually create a soil that is productive. The more total the gardener's commitment and application the greater will be his results.

To get things off to a good start, one qualification for life membership in the gardening fraternity is banishment of the word "dirt." The substance you dig and plant in— the good earth—is called "soil." Dirt is what you wash off your face.

where soil comes from

Soil is the result of nature's tearing down and putting together, tearing down of parent rock materials into minerals, then putting these particles together, in the presence of moisture, organic action, and climatic factors, into a substance that supports plant life.

Glaciers, rivers, floods, winds, and lava flows contributed initially to this breaking-down and building-up process. Low forms of plant life—tiny lichens, fungi, and bacteria—played a major role in the early stages of soil formation. Higher plants—grass, shrubs, and trees—followed. Their cumulative growing, decay, leaf litter, and root action in the soil, plus the activity of animal life, especially worms and insects, aided in creating soil.

Since the parent rock sources differ across the nation,

21

so do the soils. In many regions of the South, for example, where there is a predominance of iron, the soil is red. In the Southwest, where the land is arid, there is a high accumulation of lime (calcium carbonate), and the soil tends to be alkaline. In the Northeast, where rich forests once grew (and still do), there is abundant humus content in the soil, which is chestnut brown and usually slightly acid.

the four main ingredients

Soil is comprised of four main components—minerals, organic matter, water, and air. In average soil, the mineral component is about 50 percent of the total volume, air and water each about 20 to 25 percent, and organic content as low as 5 percent.

Minerals are inherent in the basic rock materials, as fragments varying in size from small particles such as sand to the very tiniest particles—silt and clay. The larger, nonporous particles are a kind of framework for the smaller particles, which carry out the soil's chemical and physical activities.

Organic matter, the "gluer together" of the soil, has the ability to encourage tiny, often microscopic clay humus particles to aggregate and form larger particles. This makes the soil crumbly, and easy to work, and allows it to drain well. Clay soils, without generous quantities of organic material, stick together and pack hard because they have little pore or air space. Clay soils dry out late in spring, and do not readily absorb rainfall, which runs off the surface. The other extreme—sandy soils—are large pored, drain quickly, and do not hold water readily unless sufficient organic matter is incorporated to hold moisture and nutrients.

Nearly half of soil is "space"—pore space—which is occupied by the remaining two ingredients, water and air. These pore spaces are also filled with the soil's thriving populations—the plant and animal organisms—which break down plants and animal residues into organic matter, or humus. The worms and insects initiate the physical breakdown, while the microscopic bacteria and fungi complete the decomposition and release nutrients as a by-product. The better the soil aeration, the more complete and more rapid will be the decaying process.

The tiny clay and humus particles in the soil are the

key to its fertility. These particles are charged to attract nutrient ions in solution. They hook on to the nutrients and release them when needed by plant roots.

When analyzed chemically, clay is chiefly silicon and aluminum, with small amounts of sodium, magnesium, iron, calcium, and potassium. Under microscopic examination, these clay minerals are seen to be arranged in platelike crystal structures with large spaces between, giving each clay particle great exterior surface and chemical activity. These particles are minute—anywhere from 1 micron to 200 millimicrons in diameter. They are so fine that when placed in water they remain suspended in solution almost indefinitely. This is called a "colloidal state" (from the Greek *kolla*, meaning "glue," and *oid*, meaning "like"). Homogenized milk is a good example.

Chemically, clay particles are negatively charged. They attract positively charged particles present in the soil, including hydrogen, calcium, magnesium, potash, boron, and other elements that are nutrients for plant growth. The chemical activity is influenced by the concentration of the ions and cations (positive charges) in the soil, as well as their ability to move about readily. The pH of the soil (its acid or alkaline quality) also influences the ions that remain bound and those that are released.

Much of the soil organic matter decomposed sufficiently to be called "humus" is also in a colloidal state. It, too, has the ability to absorb or "hook on" mineral ions. The humus particles are made up mainly of carbon, hydrogen, and oxygen, along with bits of other elements, mainly nitrogen, sulfur, and phosphorus. They store essential nutrients by their hooking-on process (as do the clay particles), and release them for plant growth. This hooking on prevents the nutrient ions from being leached (washed through the soil) in heavy rainfall.

Both clay and humus also have the ability to attract and hold water molecules, as well as nutrients. It is obvious that these two soil components play a vital part in the overall quality of soils for growing plants. Indeed, to put it very simply, clay and humus is where all the action is!

how soils are classified

If the mineral particles of a quantity of soil were separated, they would sort out into all sizes, from very tiny minute particles almost invisible to the eye to larger particles, or tiny rock fragments. Sorting out these various-sized mineral particles in a given amount of soil is not just an imaginary game, but the way scientists classify soils.

The very tiniest particles are clay, the next sized particles are silt, and the largest particles are sand. The sizes of these particles, which do not change, classify the soil into particular textures. For example, gardeners frequently come across directions telling them to plant in a sandy loam. A sandy loam is a type of soil texture, an ideal combination of clay, silt, and sand particles that provides an almost perfect planting medium.

One way an amateur can classify a soil for himself in a general way is to feel it. Wet your thumb and forefinger and rub the soil particles between them. A slick, slippery feel usually denotes a lot of clay particles, while a grainy, gritty feeling means many sand particles.

improving your soil

There is an old saw that says if the soil is fertile enough to support weed growth, it is fertile enough to support a vegetable garden. That's not a very reliable premise. The ugliest, barren abandoned city block will support some kind of weed growth, but this natural surge of weeds does not indicate a satisfactory location for a vegetable garden, though with the key—good soil management—even the city lot can be transformed.

The texture of the soil is the "given" which the gardener must work with, whether he lives in the city, suburbs, or country. The size of the soil particles does not change and their relative proportion to each other is the soil's texture. Little can be done to alter the soil's texture.

The better and far more economical choice is to improve the soil structure. Structure describes how all the soil particles are arranged.

The ideal soil is a crumbly, well-aerated, porous material that holds moisture yet drains well, and is nutritious for plant growth. The way to improve the soil structure is to rearrange its particles. Organic matter is the tool. To review briefly, soil particles come in three sizes: clay (small), silt (medium), and sand (large). The function of the largest particles, sand, is chiefly as a framework for the smaller particles. They are so large, they have

If a handful of soil packs in a hard ball it is too wet to dig

When a handful of soil crumbles easily the ground is ready to work

24

only a negligible function in the chemical and physical action in soils; they merely keep it porous, as do the somewhat smaller silt particles. Clay and organic matter are the soil's charged components for ion exchange.

The good earth enriched with compost is light and friable.

If the soil is sandy, addition of generous quantities of organic matter will fill in the soil pore spaces and provide more charged particle surfaces to carry on the soil nutrient activity. The organic matter will also fill in the framework of sandy soils, to give water molecules something to hang on to. Sandy soil enriched with organic matter will hold moisture.

If the soil is a heavy clay, again, the addition of generous quantities of organic matter will help. Decomposed organic matter, humus, provides the glue to aggregate the minute clay particles into larger particles. The larger the particles, the bigger the pore spaces, the better the soil aeration. The organic matter will also provide more charged surfaces for nutrient exchange.

For either sand or clay soils, the solution to changing the soil structure and improving it is organic matter. It's importance for both cannot be over emphasized. Sources are basically plant tissue—leaves, roots, plant tops, wood chips, peat, grass clippings, turned-under crops called "green manures," straw, spoiled hay, kitchen plant refuse, and so forth. These may be added to the soil directly or put on a compost pile to decompose first. (See chart on page 226.)

carbon/nitrogen ratio

The decomposition of organic matter is a complex biochemical process. The action is brought about by microorganisms—bacteria and fungi—which decompose the organic material for their own food supply, using carbon and nitrogen as energy to grow and to feed (protein synthesis). This process goes on continually in soils, as plants drop leaves, roots decay, and so forth. The microorganisms keep the balance of carbon and nitrogen somewhat constant in average soils, at a ratio of about 12:1 to 10:1. A C/N ratio change occurs when organic materials are added to the soils and the microorganisms have to work overtime to break them down.

Plant tissue—roots, stems, leaves, twigs, clippings, pods, and so forth—is about 75 percent water and 25 percent dry weight, which is mainly carbon plus hydrogen and

26

oxygen. There also are small portions of phosphorus, potassium, calcuim, sulfur, nitrogen, as well as others.

The percentage of carbon/nitrogen in the organic matter is significant, as it affects soil nutrition. Young plants, weeds, grass clippings, spent vegetable plants, leafy tops, and so forth—have low carbon content and are readily decomposed by the soil microorganisms without upsetting the natural soil C/N ratio.

But some materials have exceptionally high carbon content, particularly autumn leaves, hay, straw, and sawdust, among others. When applied to the soil, they cause the microorganisms to overwork to break them down. The activity is so extreme that they have to borrow from the soil's natural nitrogen to keep the process going. When the decomposition process is completed, the overpopulation of microbes dies down and renews the soil nitrogen balance.

Meanwhile, the plants have been starved of their much-needed nitrogen supply for growth. They become yellow and spindly. Although the depletion is only temporary, it can set back plant growth immeasurably. To compensate for this nitrogen depletion, a high nitrogen fertilizer such as blood meal, cottonseed meal, Ureaform or sodium nitrate should be added to the soil when straw, sawdust, hay, and the like have been added as organic matter. Or add high carbon materials to the soil after the growing season so that the nitrogen depletion occurs without affecting plant growth. This will also give the soil's C/N ratio time to right itself. Another idea is to compost high-carbonaceous materials and add them to the soil when well decomposed.

sheet composting

Organic matter added to the top of the soil and worked in, is called "sheet composting." Quite often this method is used in the fall months, when there is an abundance of autumn foilage and spent vegetable and flower tops to pile on the garden. They are merely tossed on top of the soil and dug or rototilled in. The soil microbes start to decompose the organic substances, and by spring they are quite well broken down into humus.

A green manure crop sown in late summer and churned under in spring with a power tiller is another quick way to add humus. Grasses such as rye, oats, and buckwheat are good green manure crops, as are any of the legumes—clover, vetch, or soybeans. The legumes have the additional value of supplying nitrogen to the soil.

Either of these methods are particularly suitable for poorly structured soil that needs great improvement. Two or three years of consistent sheet composting will have a marked effect on soil structure and productivity. Sheet composting is also a handy solution for improving soil structure where hauling quantities of compost is difficult, or where there is not sufficient manpower to do the hauling and digging.

plant
nutrition

A seed or plant placed in the soil is likely to grow, but growth must be fast and steady to produce the final goal—harvest. To speed things along, the plant must have proper nutrients.

Three environmental factors—air, water, and a favorable growing climate—are essential, in addition to good soil, for a successful garden. They provide oxygen, hydrogen, and carbon. Here the gardener must accept, more or less, what nature provides. But nourishing the soil is in your hands, and one of the arts of growing is knowing what nutrients plants need, when, and how much. Many nutrients are present in soils in varying quantities, but not all of them are always available in sufficient quantity, and may have to be added.

The vegetables must grow along at a steady rate without stress. Halts or delays in the growing will shorten, may even limit or cancel the harvest potential. Keep vegetables thriving!

The fuel to keep growth steady is proper nutrition. Plants need sixteen nutrients to grow well. They are called the essential elements, and each has a particular function in the plant's development.

The most important elements are called "macronutrients," and these, needed in great quantities, are carbon, hydrogen, oxygen, nitrogen, phosphorus, potassium, calcium, magnesium, and sulfur. The remaining seven essential elements are called "micronutrients," or "trace elements," because they are needed in lesser amounts. They are iron, manganese, copper, zinc, boron, molybdenum, and chlorine, and are generally found in good-quality soil.

the big six

Nitrogen (N) is essential for deep green color in leaves and for plant vigor. It makes leafy vegetables succulent and crisp. Nitrogen is a constituent of chlorophyll, and is abundant in the young growing parts of plants. Too much nitrogen will spur excessive vegetative growth and delay flowering and harvest; too little results in stunted growth, yellow leaves (the older leaves yellow first), weak stalks, and slow growth.

Phosphorus (P) is part of the plant's cell structure, and is necessary for rapid growth (cell division). It is also important for good root growth and development of flowers, fruit, and seed, and it increases resistance of some crops to disease. When phosphorus is lacking, plants are small and woody and do not flower well, and the leaves may have a purple tinge.

Potassium (K) plays an important role in the process of changing starch to sugars (photosynthesis). It has great influence on leaf development, as well as on root systems. Potassium is important for good harvests of root crops—potatoes, carrots, beets, and so forth. It also helps to keep water in plant cells and provides some resistance to drought. When potassium is lacking, the leaves look "fired," or dry and scorched at the edges; crops are poor quality, and plants are not vigorous.

Calcium (Ca) is needed for all vegetables, promoting early growth, vigor, and good roots. When lacking, leaves become wrinkled, plants are stunted, and growth is retarded.

Magnesium (Mg) is a constituent of chlorophyll and is important for seed development and for the formation of fat or oil in plants. Oil-rich seeds contain large quantities of magnesium. Magnesium-starved plants develop yellowing (chlorosis), usually in the lower leaves first.

Sulfur (S) is a constituent of proteins and is important in the cell chemistry of organic compounds, and spurs good root development as well. When sulfur is lacking, plants are pale green in color. Deficiencies tend to develop in dry weather.

the minor seven

The micronutrients, or trace elements—iron, manganese, copper, zinc, boron, molybdenum, and chlorine—are for the most part present in soil in sufficient amounts for vegetable growth, but their supply may usually be assured by the addition of animal manures. Nutrient action in general is linked with the plant enzymes, and serves as a catalyst so that all systems function properly. And while the functions of the micronutrients are not wholly understood by soil scientists and plant physiologists, it is known that when one or more of the minor nutrients are lacking, plants do not grow as they should. These hunger signs are most likely to show up where soils have been cropped for many years with little nutrient renewal, where pH is high, or where acid soils are heavily leached.

where nutrients come from

Of all the sixteen nutrients needed for plant growth, nitrogen is the most plentiful but also the most easily leached. Soils receive it from the air and from rainfall. Legumes—peas, beans, soybeans, and so forth—have bacteria on the root nodules that can "fix" nitrogen from the air and synthesize it into a usable form for the plants.

Soils also gain nitrogen from organic matter in the soil, but before the plants can use it, the matter must be changed by soil microorganisms from inorganic ammonium to nitrite, and finally into nitrate, a form they can use.

Three of the big six nutrients—N, P, and K—are used in such great quantities in soil that they usually must be added. Two, Ca and Mg, are supplied when the soil is limed. Sulfur is released as organic matter decomposed into humus.

The nutrient carriers are called "fertilizers." They come from two sources—organic (natural materials) and inorganic (usually synthetic sources). The organic sources are often more expensive, and not as quickly available to plants. They must be broken down first into a soluble form for plant intake. The advantage of the organics is that they supply nutrients to the soil over a prolonged period of time with little chance of burning the plant's roots. The table on page 38 lists the major organic fertilizers and the percentages of N, P, and K that they carry.

The inorganic carriers of plant nutrients are synthetics, usually manufactured to make soluble nutrients. An example is the nitrogen carrier urea, an ammoniated form of hydrogen. Other inorganic fertilizers are made from industrial by-products (slag) or mined minerals treated for solubility. The chart on page 37 lists some of the generally available inorganic carriers used in commercial fertilizers.

Choice of organic carriers or inorganic carriers is a matter for each gardener to decide. The plants will grow well with either type, although wide claims are made that organic fertilizers are better for health reasons or that synthetic fertilizers are harmful in foods.

In a Cornell University bulletin on composting, Prof. Emeritus L. G. MacDaniels notes, while discussing some gardening misconceptions:

A second fallacy is the claim that an element necessary for plant growth differs in any way when derived from organic material than when it has been derived from any other source. With few exceptions, the organic combinations of elements must be reduced to some soluble inorganic form before they can be absorbed by plants again.

In organic gardening literature, emphasis is given to the claim that vegetables and other food products that have been fertilized with inorganic chemical fertilizers are somehow harmful to human health as compared with those in which the same elements were supplied from composted or other organic materials. This is exceedingly difficult to prove and to date, despite much scientific work, there have been no results to verify this claim.

Because of their quick availability to plants when applied to soils, and their lower price when compared to organics, inorganic fertilizers are the backbone of the world's food supply. The recent energy crunch shorted supplies of natural gas affecting the nitrogen fertilizer industry and reduced mining operations have limited supply of phosphorus fertilizers. This current shortage is expected to continue for the next few years until supply catches up with demand. As a result, home gardeners may not find their favorite fertilizers at the garden centers.

fertilizer facts

Fertilizers that contain the nutrients needed for good plant growth, whether organic or inorganic, are widely sold in garden centers, supermarkets, discount centers, hardware stores, etc. If the fertilizer contains all three essential nutrients—nitrogen, phosphorus, and potassium (potash)—it is called a complete fertilizer, and is the type that should be selected for the vegetable garden.

The package label is required by law to provide particular information. It will show a set of three figures such as 10-6-4, 6-2-2-, etc. These are the percentages of nitrogen, phosphorus, and potash (in that order) contained in the package. The label will also show the carrier guarantee stating the exact form in which the nutrients are supplied. Inert filler matter makes up the full weight of the fertilizer.

The fertilizer percentages are also ratios. For example, a fertilizer 5-10-5, 8-16-8, or 10-20-10 would have a ratio of 1-2-1, 1 part nitrogen to 2 parts phosphorus to 1 part potash. A 10-pound bag of 10-20-10 would have the equivalent amount of a 20-pound bag of 5-10-5.

The inorganic fertilizers have higher analysis figures because the nutrient carriers possess larger percentages of nutrients. The synthetic nitrogen carrier urea has 45 percent nitrogen, while superphosphate, an important ingredient of commercial fertilizers, has 20 percent phosphorus. Urea, though appearing to be highly potent, releases its nitrogen over a long period and is widely used for lawns. The organic fertilizers have lower percentages. Cottonseed meal is 6-2-2-, a 3-1-1- ratio.

Fertilizers from inorganic sources or synthetic carriers will break down faster after application for quicker use by the plants. Organic fertilizers must be broken down by microbe activity first, and the nutrients are released more slowly over a longer period of time. Whatever the original source of the nutrients, whether organic or inorganic materials, the nutrients must be broken down by activity in the soil to colloidal materials in the soil solution so that they may be absorbed by the plants.

When a new garden is being started, inorganic fertilizers may be more efficient than organic, since they are more quickly available for plant use. When the soil is improved and enriched with organic matter, and a plentiful supply of soil microorganisms is present, organic fertilizers will do a fine job of maintaining soil fertility.

Also, for a quick start in the spring, some gardeners prefer to use the inorganic fertilizers for their ready availability. Spring soils are cold, and the microorganisms that break down the organic materials are sluggish in cold soil. They function better when the soil is warm.

Fertilizer choice may be predetermined by market supplies. The current crunch of available fertilizer materials may limit supplies in particular areas until production catches up with demand. Also, changes in price structures will be important guides on what to buy.

No general rule can be made about how much fertilizer to buy and apply, as rates vary with the products and nutrient ratios. The only reliable source of information will be the label on the package, so read it carefully. As a general rule of thumb, where the soil has never been cultivated for planting, 3 to 4 pounds of a general fertilizer 5-10-5 should be applied for every 100 square feet; if the garden is established and the soil has been fertilized and managed well for some years, then half that amount should be used.

To quickly rescue a crop that is showing such signs of nutrient deficiency as poor leaf color, stunting, and weak stems, the high-analysis, water-soluble fertilizers do an excellent job. Though expensive, they are worth it. Their analysis may be 20-20-20, 30-10-10, 40-20-10, and so forth. The nutrients dissolve instantly when mixed with water, and when applied to the soil they are absorbed in a matter of hours. Or the liquid mixture can be sprayed on the leaves as a foliar feeding for quick intake by the plants.

One important point to remember about choosing and using any fertilizer is that too much will spur soft, succulent growth at the expense of the crop and in excess will kill plants. Too little will result in starved, spindly rows with limited harvest. Experience and good plant sense are the best teachers, and these can be achieved by doing and learning.

how plants absorb nutrients

Once the fertilizer is in the soil, how does it help the plant grow? This is a fascinating, complicated process, but very simply, there is a lot of activity going on in the roots and soil solution or colloids. There is movement of roots toward nutrients and movement of nutrients toward roots.

Through a process of root respiration, nutrient ions close to the root membrane are energized and transported through the root-cell membrane to the inside of the root. The roots absorb preferentially what nutrient ions the plant needs. Linked to this vital activity is the interdependence of exhaust from the root respiration, in the form of carbon dioxide and other organic excretions, and the soil microorganisms that used these root wastes for their own food and energy supply.

The more favorable the soil climate, the easier it is for plants to absorb nutrients and grow. The ideal is adequately moist soil at all times, with sufficient quantities of organic matter to provide good pore spaces and aeration.

soil pH

Another vital part of nutrient availability is the soil reaction, its acidity or alkalinity. This is called, in the language of the soil scientists, its "pH reading," and it ranges, on a logarithmic scale, from 1 to 14, with 7 as the center or neutral point.

From 7 down the scale, an increasing concentration of hydrogen ions makes the soil reaction acid. Above 7, an increasing number of hydroxyl ions makes the soil alkaline. Generally, eastern soils, where there is more rainfall, tend to be acid, while western soils, which are dry, tend to be alkaline.

The ideal reading for most vegetable crops is a slightly acid soil reaction, somewhere between 6 to 6.8 (this is a good range for bacteria activity, too). Some vegetables have wide tolerance, while others are highly sensitive to acid-alkaline soils (see chart, page 37).

If the soil reaction is too extreme, either too acid or too alkaline, on either side of the pH scale, the balance of the soil chemistry is upset and some of the essential nutrients become insoluble and unavailable for plant use. Addition of fertilizers would have no effect.

For example, iron requires acid soil (pH 7 and below), in order for it to be available to plants. If the soil is too close to neutral, or pH 7, iron becomes less available to plants. (This is often seen in ericaceous plants, such as

pH REQUIREMENTS OF VEGETABLES

Acid sensitive *(grow at pH 6.0–7.0)*

Asparagus	Cauliflower	Leeks	Onions	Salsify
Beets	Celery	Lettuce	Parsnips	Spinach
Carrots	Endives	Muskmelons	Peas	

Moderately acid sensitive *(grow at pH 5.5–6.8)*

Beans	Cucumbers	Parsley	Squash	Watermelon
Broccoli	Dandelions	Peppers	Sweet corn	
Brussels sprouts	Eggplant	Pumpkins	Sweet potatoes	
Cabbage	Kale	Radishes	Tomatoes	
Chard	Kohlrabi	Rhubarb	Turnip	

Acid tolerant *(grow at pH 4.8–5.4)*

Potatoes

INORGANIC FERTILIZERS

Most commercial fertilizers for the consumer trade are sold premixed as complete fertilizers, to contain the three essential nutrients—nitrogen, phosphorus, and potash. The guaranteed percentages of the nutrient carriers appear on the package label.

These are some of the common carriers used in fertilizers, showing their nutrient percentages and derivatives.

Nitrogen carriers

Urea	42	synthetic
Ammonium sulfate	21	coke and gas by-product
Ammonium phosphate	12	synthetic
Sodium nitrate	16	saltpeter

Phosphorus carriers

Superphosphate	20	rock phosphate treated with sulfuric acid
Ammonium phosphate	48	synthetic
Basic slag	15	steel mill by-product

Potassium carriers

Muriate of potash (potassium chloride)	48	most commonly used carrier
Sulfate of potash	48	
Manure salts	25	potash salts

	percent of		
	Nitrogen	Phosphorus	Potassium
Manures * Cow (fresh)	.6	.15	.45
Horse (fresh)	.7	.25	.55
Poultry	1.5	1.0	.5
Sheep (fresh)	.5	.3	.5
Cow (dehydrated)	1	1	1
Sheep (dehydrated)	1	2	1
Natural materials Nitrogen			
Blood meal	12		
Cottonseed meal	6	1	1
Fish emulsion	5	2	2
Fish meal	10	6	2
Guano	16	10	2
Soya meal	7		
Sludge	6	4	0
Phosphorus			
Bone meal (steamed)	2	20	
Bone meal (raw)	4	10	
Ground phosphate rock		30	
Potassium			
Granite dust	0	5.0	0
Greensand		1.5	6.0
Seaweed	1.5	.6	5.0
Wood ash	0	1.0	6.0

* Note: Percentages are approximate, dependent on animal feed. Use fresh manures on soil in fall; either dig it in or allow it to weather and dig it in in spring. Fresh manures have high urine content, and can burn young seedlings and transplants.

azaleas, rhododendrons, and hollies. Yellow leaves usually mean iron deficiency.)

Phosphorus availability is a good indicator of soil conditions. Above 7.3, phosphorus combines with calcium and is unavailable to plants; below 5, it links up with iron and is again unavailable. If the pH is too low, manganese and aluminum reach toxic concentrations, and if it is too high, harmful salts develop.

The only way to know accurately what the soil reaction is, is to have a soil test made. Corrections can then be made to adjust the pH reading with lime applications.

Inexpensive (under $2) home soil-test kits are available to test soil for pH. Most of these kits include a test tube, lime solution, and a color guide. A sample of soil is wetted with the solution, and when the particles settle, the liquid color is matched with the color guide to give an approximate pH reading.

There are also elaborate amateur soil-test kits available for home use, ranging in cost up to $30. These include testing materials for nitrogen, phosphorus, and potassium as well.

Professional soil-testing services are also available. The most accessible is usually the state Cooperative Extension service, either at the state university or in the local county office. (Addresses of the Cooperative Extension Services for each state are listed on page 274.) These offices usually charge a nominal fee for soil testing, and quite often they will supply kits for mailing soil samples to the laboratory.

For those who want to make their own soil tests, the taking of an accurate soil sample is essential to get a practical reading. The following instructions for taking an accurate soil sample for testing are mailed to home gardeners by Rutgers University.

1. The best time to sample soils is when the moisture content is right for tilling.

2. Use a trowel, spade, auger, or soil tube, and a clean pail, to obtain thin vertical slices or cores of soil from the surface to a depth of 6 to 7 inches at ten to fifteen places throughout a given area. The number of slices or borings may be reduced to five to ten in areas less than 100 square feet.

3. Insert trowel or spade into the soil to a depth of 6 to 7 inches. Remove soil and throw it aside, then take a ½-inch slice of soil and keep it on the trowel or spade.

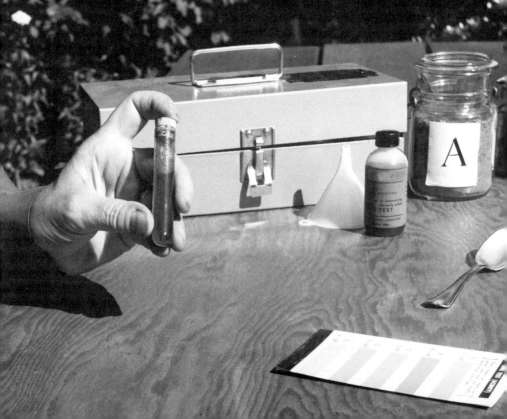

*To test soil, an
accurate sampling
must be made for
a correct analysis.*

Use a knife to cut from this slice on the trowel or spade
a 1-inch core, from top to bottom, and place it in a clean
bucket or container. Repeat this procedure at each of the
ten to fifteen places.

4. Sample separately areas that have received different
lime and/or fertilizer treatments. Also sample separately
areas used for different types of plants. For example, keep
samples taken from lawn areas separate from samples
taken from flower and shrub areas. Similarly, samples
from rhododendron, azalea, and other broadleaf ever-
green areas should be kept separate from other shrub
areas.

5. Where poor growth exists, separate samples should be
taken from both good and bad areas, if possible, and
submitted separately.

6. Do not sample areas that have been limed or fertilized
within the past few weeks unless trouble is evident.

7. If soil is wet when taken, it should be spread out on
a clean paper to air dry. After air drying, mix thoroughly
the soil taken from the different places for each sample
and put ½ to 1 pint in a plastic bag. Seal with a rubber
band.

8. Do not put more than one sample in each sample bag.

*The pH reading is
made by allowing the
wetted sample to
settle and matching
with a color on the
chart.*

If the test indicates that the soil is too acid, this can be
corrected by adding ground limestone (calcium carbonate). If the limestone has a high quantity of magnesium,
it is called "dolomitic limestone." Both are used for cor-
recting soil acidity.

Generally, soils in the humid temperate regions, where
there is ample rainfall, tend to be acid because the rainfall leaches the calcium and magnesium, which must be
replaced. Lime is primarily a soil pH corrector but is also
a fertilizer because it contains calcium and sometimes
magnesium. It makes the soil more efficient by releasing
the elements needed for plant growth, and hooking up
other nutrients that might be harmful.

If the test shows that the soil is extremely acid, its pH
level will have to be raised gradually over a period of
several years, as too much lime applied at one time is
harmful to soil bacteria. An average application rate is
35 to 50 pounds per 1,000 square feet. The soil test
report will state specifically how much lime should be
applied. Use a spreader to apply the lime accurately
and rake it in afterward. Lime and fertiilzer can be applied at the same time.

Gypsum (hydrous calcium sulfate) or land plaster is

41

recommended for use on soils in the arid regions of the western states. There soils tend to have excessive salt concentrations (sulfates, chlorides, nitrates) and are called "saline," or they have a high concentration of sodium and are called "alkali;" some soils have both. These concentrations adversely affect crops. Adding gypsum to them puts them in working order. The soil is unplugged to permit leaching of the harmful salts.

When gypsum is added to soils in other parts of the country, it supplies calcium but does not increase pH. However, gypsum does have some beneficial effect on flocculation, or lumping, in paticular soil situations.

better flavor and nutrition?

Those who raise their own vegetables also say that they taste better and are more nutritious for the family. There is certainly good reason for the vegetables to taste better. They are picked at their prime of perfection, maybe minutes or hours before they are consumed. Market produce may be harvested days before it is consumed, and shipped long distances as well. Some natural flavor is bound to be lost.

The backyard gardener is also master of his own variety choices, and he can pick those which have the flavor he likes. But taste quality is a nebulous subject to analyze and a difficult one to measure, since flavor depends on a number of physical and chemical attributes, as well as the factors of personal preferences and prejudices. Only recently have plant breeders and horticulturists turned their efforts to quality, particularly flavor, and great strides will be forthcoming in pinning down this nebulous area in the pleasures of eating vegetables.

Wide claims are also made by enthusiasts that foods organically grown taste better and are more nutritious. Food stores that sell these particular foods gainfully charge higher prices for them, and the public responds with increasing demand for more. This question has been given extensive attention, and there is no proof that foods grown without synthetic fertilizers are better for you. A recent scientific status summary by the Institute of Food Technologists reported in *Food Technology* that

Organically grown foods are identical in nutrition to those grown by conventional methods using inorganic

42

chemicals. There is no scientific evidence that can demonstrate any difference.

Soil improvement can increase the yield and size of crops, but not the composition of the plant in regard to its major nutritional characteristics.

The report goes on to say:

Basic to any discussion as to difference in the quality of nutrient sources is the fact that both organic and inorganic nutrients must be in a soluble state before a plant can utilize them. Oxygen is the only element that is used directly by plants. All other elements must be in an ionic, or soluble form, before they can be metabolized and assimilated by the plant. The essential components of commercial fertilizers are in this form already; organic fertilizers must be converted by microorganisms into their inorganic components such as potassium, phosphorus and nitrogen. These nutrients are absorbed by the plant in soluble form and their source—whether from animal waste or a compounded fertilizer— cannot be identified.

proper tools

A few tools—spade, rake, hoe and trowel—are adequate for basic garden needs. Then, as the months and years progress and different needs occur, additional gadgets and tools will start to fill the garage, basement, or tool shed.

Before any tool is purchased, shop around a bit to see what is available and compare prices. Tools range in quality from discount bargain lines to high-priced luxury models. Somewhere in between, most gardeners will find something suitable.

Cheap tools are worthless. They break, dull, rust, and have to be replaced once or twice, doubling or tripling the initial cost. Look for quality construction and good balance, and rely on established brand names. Stainless steel tools with molded plastic handles are a good buy. They should last a lifetime with proper care.

The following should put the vegetable gardener to work:

spade, d-handled fork, or shovel This tool, in whatever model chosen, will be the first one used to turn over the soil. Choice of spade, 4-pronged fork or shovel model depends on individual tastes and requirements to do the job, though the spade with its sharp end is usually preferred. Those who are planning sizable compost piles may like the fork style, as it most easily "bites" into the compact mass of compost for mixing and turning. Look for quality styling and well-balanced handles, smooth finish and sturdy steel construction.

metal rake A strong, long-handled rake is essential to smooth out turned over ground, to clear out stones and pebbles, and to break up soil clods. Rakes are made with either a bow or flat top, with 12 to 14 teeth. Some prefer the flat top rake, since it easily flops over for making seed drills at planting time. (Incidentally, this heavy metal rake should never be used on turf to rake up grass clippings. Only a soft-tined metal or bamboo grass rake should be used on lawns.)

hoe Hoe shopping is fun, as they come in all sorts of shapes, sizes, models and lengths of handles. There are ladies' hoes and children's hoes; heart-shaped, flat-bottomed, or triangular-shaped hoes; and double-ended half-hoes or two-pronged weeding hoes. The hoe will be used for two essentials—opening and covering seed drills at planting time and cultivating the soil to keep down weeds. For cultivating, a special personal preference is the scuffle hoe. This is a unique, flat-bottomed slicing hoe that is pushed along the surface of the soil, knocking off weeds at their "necks" as the hoe is pushed back and forth between rows. Only the top surface of the soil is cultivated, and there is no chance of digging deeply and breaking off shallow-rooted vegetables.

cultivator For most gardeners, the hoe is sufficient for loosening the soil, but for a very large garden, some may prefer to invest in a long-handled claw type cultivator or a wheel hoe.

watering can A sturdy gallon-sized watering can with a removable spray head or "hose" is good to have at transplanting time to wet down plants. And with the spray head attached, a watering can is also handy for wetting down seedlings in a small garden. (For a larger garden, a hose makes better sense.) Watering cans come in metal or sturdy plastic, which is preferable because of its light weight.

hand tools A sturdy trowel and hand cultivator are good investments. The trowel is for transplanting time. There are many models, with wooden or molded handles and everything from very narrow to very wide blades. Again, choice is left to individual likes and dislikes. Since the trowel is one of the basic garden tools, invest in a sturdy one; it should provide decades of good service. The hand cultivator is useful when working around the vegetable

1 spade   ⎫
2 fork   ⎬ one of these
3 shovel   ⎭
4 bow rake   ⎫
5 straight rake ⎬ one of these
6 triangular hoe
7 scuffle hoe
8 trowel
9 hand cultivator
10 long handled cultivator
11 string and stakes
12 watering can
13 compressed air sprayer
14 hand duster

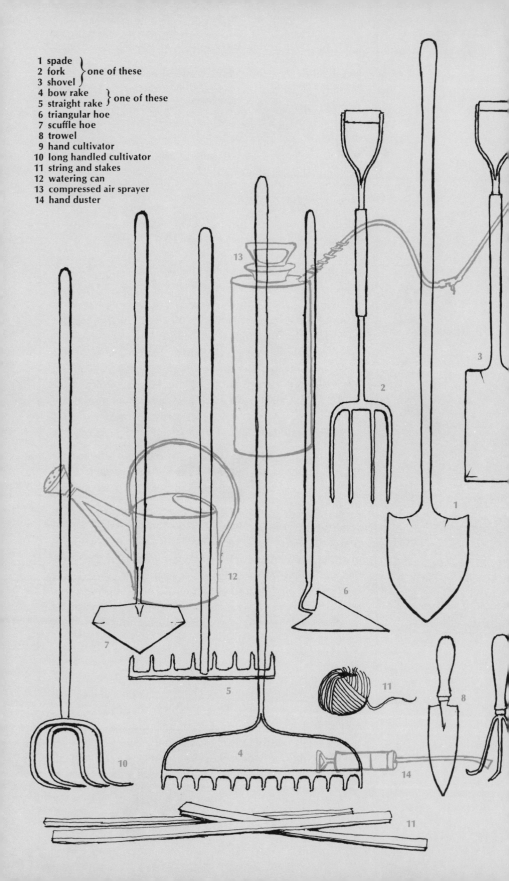

patch, even a large one, to scratch up tough soil or break up clods for some light replanting.

strings and stakes If anyone takes particular pride in his vegetable garden, as most any gardener does, a straight alignment of rows is rather impressive. For marking out the long garden rows evenly, these two measurers are indispensable. A sawed-off bamboo pole is handy, along with a ball of serviceable string. (And a good old-fashioned yardstick will help, too!) For very small gardens, use the back end of a rake and tamp it down lightly with your foot to mark the seed row.

Some other equipment will surely be needed as the summer moves along. A hose with an adjustable nozzle will help. And if the insect or disease problems get out of control, a sprayer or duster is handy. Small power sprayers (rechargeable) are a major investment at the start, but convenience and efficient operation make them worth the price. For very large gardens, many may prefer the hose-end jar sprayers, which do an efficient job. Another type is the hand-pump compression sprayer, with adjustable nozzle, which comes in large 1½-gallon or small ½-gallon models. The simplest duster is the plunger type, which holds about 1 pound of dry material and comes with a detachable extension tube with a swivel nozzle.

Probably the one investment that most gardeners do not think of initially, but use the most, is a garden cart or wheelbarrow. It has innumerable uses, and once a gardener owns one, he usually can't get along without it.

Power tractors and rototillers can be rented for a nominal sum. And if several home gardeners in a neighborhood want to churn up their vegetable gardens about the same time, it may be economical to join together and rent equipment. A rototiller does a swift efficient job of churning up a garden plot to make it ready for planting if the area is large enough to warrant the charges. Or it may be possible to hire someone to come in with his power equipment to turn over the soil. This is the hardest part of getting the garden ready, and any steps to make it easier are worth the investment. Buying this type of equipment is sensible for large property owners who will use it enough to make paying the price worthwhile.

And finally, just a word or two on tool care. Keep them clean. This will lengthen their life. Keep paper towels or old rags handy, and after each use wipe off the soil. Many gardeners like to wipe their tools often with oiled rags to ward off rust. But be careful about letting old oiled rags lie about carelessly, since they are a potential fire hazard. One thorough oiling at the end of the season before storing should be sufficient. And if rust does start, it can easily be removed with commercial rust removers and steel wool.

starting seed indoors

A number of vegetables take so long to grow from seed to harvest, they need a head start indoors so they will mature before frost. The best-known long-season vegetable is the tomato. Few gardeners live in regions where they can sow tomato seed outdoors. Besides, tomatoes get a better start if plants are set out rather than seeded directly. Other long-season crops needing a head start are peppers, eggplant, head lettuce, the cabbage family, and melons.

Another reason for starting seed indoors is to have a greater choice of varieties. Garden centers do stock generous selections of transplants for sale in the spring, but they will not always have specific varieties. The only way to guarantee choice of a particular variety is to grow your own.

Then there is the challenge of starting seed indoors. Many gardeners are fascinated by watching tiny seedlings develop. Finally, when the tomatoes and melons are ready for picking at the end of the summer, there is the happy satisfaction of knowing they were home grown all the way.

There are several musts for starting seed indoors; otherwise don't try. The first and formost essential is sun—sun all day, if possible, or at least during the mid-day hours. Once germinated, the tiny seedlings must grow rapidly, and without enough sunlight to spur them along they become weak, spindly, and elongated.

49   Those who have greenhouses or a sun room or closed

sun porch have an ideal environment for starting seedlings. Or choose a room with southern exposure and no trees outdoors to block the full light from the sun.

An alternative, is a setup of fluorescent lights. Then seedlings can even be grown in the basement, or whereever there is space.

Another must for seed starting indoors is growing space. The seedlings are teeny when they come up, but they grow rapidly and fill a lot of table space once they start developing. They are messy to keep, as water sometimes spills over or the containers seep moisture, so avoid placing containers on the family's good furniture. An old card table or two, or temporary growing shelves, are safer.

The growing space must also be warm. Seedlings need the same growing temperatures as many tender house plants, 70 to 72 degrees during the day, with about a 10-degree drop at night. Since seedlings are growing in the early spring months when winds and sudden cold snaps occur, be sure there are no seeping drafts of cool air from windows—these could mean ruin.

when to start

Not too soon. A too-early start for seedlings is probably the mistake most often made, on the theory that the sooner the seed is started indoors, the sooner the crop will be ready for harvest outdoors. Not so.

Seedlings will grow rapidly after germination, up to a point. But they eventually slow down as the roots fill the confines of the growing space and the low-light levels limit their growth. Too early a start is really a setback, then, for seedlings become weak and spindly and have to readjust when set out in the garden before full-scale growth continues.

Start the seedlings at the recommended time so that the young plants are thriving and bursting with growth when they are set outdoors. They adjust readily in a short period and go on growing well.

A general guide for how soon to start vegetables indoors is simply calculated: Look up the number of weeks required for starting seedlings and count back from the average date of the last killing frost for your particular area. Most of these seedling vegetables are sensitive to cool weather and soil, and cannot be transplanted outdoors until the weather is settled. Exceptions are members of the cabbage family and lettuce, which can be planted a bit sooner.

The number of weeks needed for starting seed indoors:

Cabbage family	4–5
Eggplant	6–7
Lettuce (head)	4
Melons	2–3
Onions	2–3
Peppers	6–7
Tomatoes	5–6

planting

Seed catalogs and garden centers sell all sorts of equipment for starting seed indoors. There are peat pots, soil mixes, miniature greenhouses, planting trays, heating cables, fluorescent light setups, and plastic pots. At the other end of the spectrum are the planters home made from plastic and aluminum food containers.

You can be as plain or as fancy as you wish. Only one thing must be insisted upon, and that is cleanliness. Seedlings are subject to a devastating fungus called damping-off disease, that knocks out seedlings overnight. One day they will be bright and perky; the next morning, toppled over and dead.

Another form of the fungus rots the sprouting seed before it ever pops above ground. The only practical way to prevent this problem is to use clean containers and sterile planting mediums—seed starting mixes or potting soil for young seedlings. Never use soil straight from the garden.

The most widely available and relatively inexpensive seed-starting medium is vermiculite. This sterile product is made by heating vermiculite ore (a form of mica) to a high temperature until it swells and pops into tiny granules, with many air cells, that will hold many times their weight in water. The medium is completely sterile, and an excellent support for tiny seedling roots. Seedlings cannot be grown in vermiculite for very long, as it has no nutrient value. Plants must either be fed regularly with water-soluble fertilizers or transplanted to soil when large enough.

This soil must also be sterilized to be sure it is free

of the damping-off fungus. Potting soils are widely available at garden stores, and are usually sterilized. Check the package label to be sure before buying. There now are available seed-starting mixes made up of inert materials such as peat, vermiculite, and perlite, with nutrients added so the medium will grow the seed once it has started.

If a great number of seedlings are to be started indoors, a home-mix batch of seed starting material may be more economical. Here is a recipe called Cornell Mix, recommended by the Harris Seed Company and based on research done by Cornell University. For 1 peck, use:

4 quarts no. 2 grade horticultural vermiculite
4 quarts shredded peat moss
1 tablespoon 20 percent powdered superphosphate
2 tablespoons ground limestone
1½ tablespoons 33 percent ammonium nitrate or
4 tablespoons 5-10-5 fertilizer

These ingredients should be mixed thoroughly. This mixture is completely sterile, free of fungus organisms, light, and porous.

These planting mixes are very dry and fluffy. Whether packaged or home mixed, moisten them well before using. A hand mister is a practical way to dampen them down without oversoaking, or you can open the bag without breaking it, pour some water in, and knead the bag to mix the moisture through.

If buying soil for seedlings is not possible, then garden soil may be used if it is sterilized first. To do this, place it in a shallow roasting pan and bake it in the oven for an hour at a low temperature (below 200). This kills any damping-off fungus. The odor is not too pleasant, so try to bake soil on a mild day when you can air out the kitchen.

One of the most practical developments for starting seed are pressed peat containers. These are made from peat moss, mixed with nutrients, which is dampened, pressed into pot forms, and dried. Then they are filled with soil. The peat pots prevent transplanting shock because they are broken down by soil moisture and the pressure of seedling roots pushing out through them as the vegetables grow. By the end of the gardening season, these peat pots are usually well decomposed.

There are, also, cubes of pressed peat, which are

Pots made of compressed peat.

Discs of pressed peat swell to potlike cylinders when soaked in water.

Cubes of pressed peat for seedlings.

wetted for seed planting; also popular are flattened discs of pressed peat that swell to a small cylinder when soaked briefly in water. All have the same function: to avoid transplanting shock when seedlings are set out in the garden.

The simplest seed-starting containers are from the kitchen: the best are aluminum foil frozen-food trays. Simply poke a few drainage holes in the bottom of these trays with an ice pick after they are thoroughly cleaned. Other handy starting containers are cottage cheese dishes and the bottom halves of milk cartons, ice cream cartons, and plastic gallon bleach bottles. All must have drainage holes, which can be made with an ice pick, to allow excess water to run off.

Fill these cleaned containers with vermiculite to a depth of several inches, and use a separate container for each kind of seed. Lightly sprinkle seed on top of the vermiculite by tapping the end of the packet. If the seed is large, such as melon seed, cover it well with a thin layer of vermiculite. The finer seeds, such as lettuce and tomatoes, just need a light sprinkling of vermiculite.

Carefully place the seed pan in a tray of water. The moisture will seep up through the drainage holes in the bottom and soak into the vermiculite. When the vermiculite is wetted through to the top, lift the pan out of the water and set it aside to drain for a short time. Then insert it into a plastic bag, tie shut, and place it in a warm, out-of-the-way place, away from strong light.

Check the tray every few days to see if the seedlings are popping up. When they are, take the tray out of the plastic bag and put it in full sunlight. The plastic bag solves the problem of keeping seed moist for good sprouting. The single watering after planting is sufficient until germination, since the vermiculite has such great water-holding capacity. When placed in full sun, seedlings must be checked daily to be sure they are moist. If not, water gently.

An alternate method is to plant a few seeds directly in peat discs. The easiest way is to poke a hole in the center with a pencil and drop two or three seeds in. Again, water after planting from the top with a spouted watering can (the kind used for house plants is fine). Line all the individual peat pots up in an aluminum food tray, cake pan, or something similar, and again place in a plastic bag to keep the moisture even until the seed germinates.

After watering seed pan, made from aluminum-foil frozen food tray, insert it in a plastic bag and tie shut to keep uniformly moist.

When seedlings germinate, remove tray from the plastic bag and place in full sun.

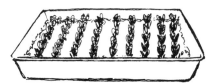

Then remove the bag and place the seedlings in full sun. Check daily for moisture needs.

For those who want to be fancier, seed catalogs can supply a fine assortment of seed-starting equipment. Those who plan to do an extensive amount of seed starting indoors year after year may find these a practical investment. For example, there are heated trays to provide bottom heat and spur germination. Also available are seed-starting kits, which have plastic trays filled with pre-planted seedling cubes. To start them growing, merely punch a hole in the plastic cover, water and place away from light until the seedlings start. These are fun for children, especially. Seedsmen have had trouble with the packaging of these kits, however, as the seed is sometimes jostled about, limiting germination.

growing

Once the seedlings have germinated, the trick is to keep them thriving. To insure this, sunlight is the key. Turn the seedlings every day, as they lean toward the light; turning will keep their stems growing straight.

Check the trays or pots daily to be sure they are moist to the touch. Be very careful about overwatering peat pots and vermiculite. These materials hold substantial quantities of moisture, and evaporation varies with each growing environment. In an ideal damp greenhouse atmosphere, for example, these mediums stay quite moist for a longer period of time than they would in a dry, heated apartment with little humidity. So check daily, but don't overwater.

54

Seedlings planted in vermiculite will have to be transplanted to soil. They are large enough to handle when the second pair of true leaves appears. The first leaves are the simple seedling leaves, quite different in appearance from the true leaves of the vegetable.

When the second pair of true leaves form, the seedlings can be pushed gently out of the vermiculite with a pencil, one at a time, and placed in planting trays or peat pots filled with sterile soil. Never hold the seedling by the stem, but by one of its leaves. And don't shake the vermiculite off the roots; just put the whole glob of vermiculite and roots into a hole poked in the soil with a pencil. Then tuck in the roots carefully with the pencil or press ever so gently with the thumbs and water well. Keep seedlings that have been transplanted out of sunlight for a day or so until they are adjusted.

There will be no need to transplant seedlings if the seed was sown directly in peat pots. They will continue growing until it is time to plant them outdoors. But more than one of the seeds planted will germinate, and there is growing space for one plant only. Seek out the strongest seedling and with a scissors, cut off the others at the base of the stems to avoid disturbing the delicate root system of the main seedling.

From here on, the seedlings will have to be kept growing along at a steady rate. They should do very nicely if the growing climate is right—enough sunlight, adequate warmth and moisture. If for any reason the seedlings begin to look yellow and thin, they might need a boost with water-soluble house plant fertilizer, but be very careful to apply at only *half-strength*. Once or twice should be enough. If the seedlings appear to be thriving too rapidly and growing too large, they can be held back slightly by watering less often.

fluorescent lights

For those who have the space, but not the sunshine, fluorescent lights are a fine solution. Seed catalogs and garden centers have prefab setups, ranging from the very simplest—a small stand with adjustable legs to support the reflector and two 20-inch tubes—to the fancy wheel carts and tiered stands that can be used as display areas for growing all sorts of plants indoors. One advantage in growing seedlings under fluorescent lamps—

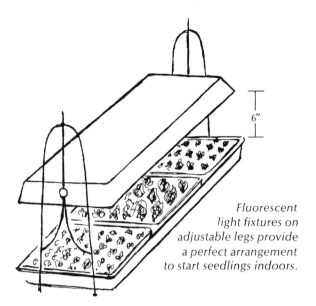

Fluorescent
light fixtures on
adjustable legs provide
a perfect arrangement
to start seedlings indoors.

there is always sunshine; no cloudy days interfere. The lights are turned on each day, giving the seedlings the high light levels and warmth needed for rapid growth.

These stands can be placed in the basement or any room where there is space and sufficient room warmth. Plastic nest trays can be bought to fit under the lamps and hold the seedling planters. Or waterproof trays found around the house can be used to hold the seedlings.

Planting and care are essentially the same for plants under lights as for those growing in the sun, but the seedlings may dry out a bit faster with the artificial light source. Also, since the light is overhead, they will grow up straight, and there is no need to turn them.

There are many brands of horticultural fluorescent lamps on the market. These are slightly more expensive than the standard fluorescents. If they cannot be located, then seedlings can be grown just as well under a combination of Cool White and Daylight fluorescents.

Plant the seeds in the vermiculite seedling tray in the same manner as described for growing the plants in sunlight. Keep the tray in plastic bags and do not place under the lights until the seedlings germinate.

After germination, the seed tray should be placed fairly close to the lights—about 4 inches above the seed-

As soon as the weather is settled and the nights are warm, tomato seedlings can be set outdoors. An old muffin tin will support peat pots while the seedlings are growing indoors.

56

lings at first, then adjusted, as they grow, to 5 or 6 inches above the leaves. The seedlings will grow along rapidly, and will be ready for transplanting in a short period of time.

Keep the lights on for 14 to 16 hours each day. If the plants become leggy and spindly, raise the height of the lights or give the seedlings a half-strength application of water-soluble plant food. Misting each morning with plain water is also helpful to keep humidity high.

Seedlings grow so well under fluorescent light, they may be ready a week or so sooner for planting outdoors. A few experiments each year will guide the timing for future plantings of seedlings indoors.

hardening off

Seedlings cannot go directly from their sheltered indoor life to the great outdoors. They must be conditioned first. This process is called "hardening off," and is merely a gradual adjustment to a new growing environment.

Start about 10 days before the plants are to be set outdoors. During the day put them outside, not in direct sun, but in partial shade, and be sure to bring them back indoors well before sundown. Continue this routine daily, gradually placing them in more direct sunlight. Check them for water, too, as they will be transpiring rapidly. Then perhaps a night or two before the plants will be set in the garden, leave them out all night, on steps or on a porch, where they will not be directly on the ground. Be sure they are watered well before they are set in the ground.

preparing
the soil

The initial soil preparation for a new vegetable garden is most important. If it is done thoroughly in the beginning, preparation in future years will be ever so much easier.

The whole purpose of preparing the soil is to make an open, softly textured growing space that is fertile, and where roots can take hold and boost sturdy growth. Turning over the ground also provides some aeration and mixing. The raking that follows evens out soil clods and makes a smooth surface for seed. When this process is repeated over the years, the ground becomes soft and friable.

When to start? Almost every seed packet and garden book uses the phrase "as soon as the ground can be worked." This means when the soil is sufficiently dried out from spring rains and melting snows to be dug. If soil, especially heavy clay soil, is worked too soon, it develops clods and packs and causes future troubles.

The best way to know when the soil can be worked is the old farmer's test. Take a handful of soil and squeeze it, then open your hand and touch the soil ball with your fingers. If it falls apart easily, the ground is sufficiently dried out to work. If the soil stays in a tight wet ball, be patient and wait until the sun and wind dry it more thoroughly.

Sometimes springs are rainy and wet or heavy snows are late in melting and planting is delayed. To bypass this problem, dig the vegetable garden, new or old, in fall.

The soil will dry out faster in spring if it is open and lying fallow. All that will need to be done for spring planting is a good stiff raking and the addition of some fertilizer.

Before doing any digging, measure off the size of the garden plot. Although many gardeners think they have a good eye for digging straight lines, it is amazing how many times they err and the garden plot ends up in strange shapes. Use a ball of string and some stakes to mark off the area to be dug. Or take a tape measure to mark the square corners so there will at least be a goal to aim for. Any way helps, but don't rely on dead reckoning, especially if the vegetable garden is a plot taken out of the formal lawn area.

Soil should be dug and turned over to spade depth, at least 8 inches. This will provide a good, deep area for the young roots to take hold as they grow. As they mature and become stronger, they can penetrate the deeper, harder subsurface. This top layer will also be well worked with organic matter and nutrients to spur initial growth.

For a small plot, the spade is handiest for turning over the soil. Some may find the easiest way is to tackle the job in sections, a little each day. Make the spade cut straight down to get the deepest length of soil and flop it over. If a piece of lawn is being cut up, cut down through the sod and turn it over. Chop it up with the spade or digging fork and toss aside roots.

A large plot is more efficiently turned with a power tiller. These can be rented for a nominal sum, borrowed from a neighbor perhaps, or hired from a local garden service. Small home tractors with plow and disc attachments also do a serviceable job of turning larger plots over.

If there is a choice, the power tiller does the best job, especially if a lawn area is being used for the new vegetable garden. The churning, chopping action of the blades does an excellent job of slicing up the turf so that it decomposes readily to supply organic matter to the soil. The machine should be operated at slow speed to enable the blades to dig in and cut the turf. Fall is an excellent time to rototill turf; this allows time for the overturned sod to break down to humus.

The new vegetable garden will need fertilizer, organic matter, and probably lime to get the crops off to a good

To dig the garden press down spade t full depth and tur soil ove

start. If the sod has been turned over in the fall, add these materials in the spring; otherwise they leach out with winter rains and melting snows.

If the digging is done in the spring, add these improvement materials after the initial heavy digging. Place them on top of the turned-over soil and lightly dig or rototill them into the top layers of the soil.

A general all-purpose fertilizer, such as 5-10-5, is a good choice for most soils. Apply it over the ground with a spreader or lightly broadcast at the rate of 4 to 5 pounds per 100 square feet. In the humid regions, where soils tend to be acid, lime at the rate of 4 to 5 pounds per 100 square feet is a good idea, unless a soil test shows otherwise. If compost or humus is available inexpensively, add this on top of the fertilizer and lime, or buy peat moss to make a 2- to 3-inch layer. Then churn the three into the soil at one time and rake it level.

Manures are also excellent soil improvers for vegetable gardens. Fresh manure has a high urine content, which would burn young seedlings, so add it to the soil in the fall and turn it under. By spring it will be well decomposed, adding nutrients to the soil.

If well-rotted manure is available, it can be added to the soil just before planting time. Use it at the rate of 1 bushel for every 50 square feet, and add a handful of superphosphate for each bushel to balance the nutrients.

Green manure is an excellent way to improve very poor soils. These are vegetative crops sown on top of the soil at the end of the growing season or in late summer. They are allowed to grow through fall and remain until spring, when they are turned under. Farmers use this method to improve soils that need organic matter, better drainage, and water retention. Some of the best green-manure crops are rye, soybeans, clover, and vetch. The seed is sold in rural areas or at major garden centers in large metropolitan areas. The crops can be planted in the fall if the first-year garden is dug at that time and left to be turned under again in spring. The green-manure crop should not be thought of as a replacement for fertilizer, lime, and peat or compost, but rather as an addition.

For an established vegetable garden that needs soil improvement, green-manure crops can be sown in between the rows toward the end of the growing season. As each crop is matured and the row cleared, it also can be sown

with seed. This makes the garden look untidy and un-
kempt, and neighbors may be curious as to what is going
on, but the rewards of digging in this nitrogen-providing
organic matter are well worth it. If done consistently
over several years, even the worst soils can be greatly
helped.

To sum up, soil preparation of the established garden
can be done in fall or spring. If fresh manure is available,
dig it in in the fall, then in spring add a light application
of the fertilizer of your choice, plus a stiff raking to mix
it in well. This should suffice preparation for planting.
For spring preparation, well-rotted manure can be added.
Add some superphosphate and lime if needed, plus fertilizer. Rake the layers evenly over the soil and dig or
rototill. Rake smooth and the ground is ready for planting.

An alternate to digging and plowing is the top-mulch
garden, a no-work scheme. One of the leading enthusiasts
for this type of garden is the well-known author Ruth
Stout.

Very simply, the system is a sheet composting on top
of the soil to provide a well-decomposed, light, airy bed
of organic matter for planting. The initial mulch is a thick
layer of spoiled hay placed on top of the garden or even
turf, if a new garden is being started. It decomposes,
working down through the turf layer. Eventually, with
the addition of some nutrients, more hay layers, and
kitchen wastes—peelings, egg shells, leafy tops, and so
forth—there results a light, airy layer of organic matter
for planting. Some gardeners in regions of heavy clay
soils have found this method not too satisfactory, as
drainage is poor and the soil remains chilled late in the
planting season. But for those who like to experiment and
try new systems, this is a unique way to plant.

A short cut to makin
a seed furrow is th
back of a rake handl
pressed into the soi

planting and cultivating

E xcept for harvesting, planting the seeds and seedlings is the best part of vegetable gardening. It's
exciting when the time finally comes to get started. Plan
to plant as much of the garden as possible at a time to
avoid excess tracking over the preciously prepared
ground. Some gardeners use boards to walk on to prevent
trampling, but this isn't really necessary. After planting,
the spaces between the rows should be hoed lightly to
open them up again, so they do not pack hard.

When planting, don't forget to use that planting plan
you worked on so carefully during the winter months.
That is the blueprint for the harvest. Either take it outdoors when planting or study it carefully so you know
exactly what goes where.

Follow the guides on when to plant carefully: Hardy
seeds in cold weather—radishes, beets, lettuce, onions,
peas—and the more tender kinds when the soil warms
up—beans, corn, okra and carrots. And don't forget that
trick of planting partial rows so that all the harvest does
not come at once, but gradually.

There are two important tools for planting, a hoe and
rake. Remember that ever-so-handy ball of string, yardstick, and stakes to keep the rows straight.

Start at one end of the garden and work out a planting pattern to avoid as much tramping on the soil as
possible. The spacing between rows is for two purposes—
to allow the vegetables enough room to grow and to

64

allow you enough space for walking in between when tending and harvesting.

The first row will be the measuring rod for all the other rows that are planted. Measure off the exact location with the yardstick, then put in the two stakes and stretch the line between. If the soil is lumpy and full of clods, rake it over again smoothly to make as fine a seed bed as possible, and of course, always remove any stones.

If the seed to be sown is very fine, such as lettuce, it helps to go across the row first and pulverize the soil by rubbing it between your hands. Then, with the edge of the hoe very gently trace a thin line alongside the string. This is a drill, or open row ready to receive the seed. Beginners have the habit of making their drills too deep and burying the seed too deeply. For fine seed, sometimes it is easier to make a drill by laying the handle of the hoe along the row and stepping on it gently to mark a slight depression in the soil.

Now for the seed. Again, moderation. Not too much, yet enough to fill the row with young plants. There are two easy ways to sow the seed. Tear a corner off the seed packet and gently tap the seed into the row, a little at a time, at the correct spacing marked on the seed packet. Or pour some of the seed into your hand, then pick out a few at a time and sprinkle them in the row by rubbing them between your thumb and forefinger.

There is no need to be concerned whether the seed is upside down or not. Seeds know all about top and bottom. Roots naturally grow downward and leaves upward, a response called "geotropism."

Keep the planted row open until the entire length, or as much of the row as planned, is filled. Check to see if there are any gaps and fill in carefully, then cover the row. For fine seed, just take your fingers and very carefully push some soil over the row and tap it firmly with the palm of your hand.

If the seeds are larger, such as bean, pea, and corn, the drill is made 1 or 2 inches deep. Merely pull the corner of the hoe along the side of the string to open a small trench for the seed. Then, one by one, space the large seed along the row according to the spacing marked on the packet. When this row is filled, check for gaps, then cover the seed by carefully pulling the hoe over the row at a side angle to fill in the drill. Finally, take the back

67

of the rake and tamp it firmly across the top of the row for a last tuck-in.

If necessary, the rows can be marked at the end by poking a stick in the ground to show the exact location. If the seed packet has been emptied, some people like to put it on the stick as a marker for the row.

Once the seed is planted, moisture is essential for good germination. Planting just before a soft, gentle rain, if you can manage it, is a good omen for a good harvest. But if the rain is scant after planting, be sure the hose is out and used. Lightly sprinkle the soil surface each day until the seed germinates. Then keep a watch over the soil from then on to be sure it is moist enough to keep the young seedlings thriving.

Some seed seems to take forever to germinate. Carrot is notoriously slow, especially when planted early in the season. It seems to germinate better when the soil is warmer. Radish seed can be mixed with the carrot to mark the row, but this does not always work, since the radish seed is so much larger and heavier; the row may turn out to be blocks of radish seed with sparse plantings of carrots here and there. Some mix sand or soil with fine seed to aid planting.

The later the seed is sown in spring when the soil is warmer, the faster germination will be. Leaf lettuce, for example, may take 10 days to germinate in cool spring soil. When sown in warmer soil, it germinates in 4 to 5 days.

If there is no sign of seed germination in 2 to 3 weeks, the seed may have rotted in the ground. This often happens if the early planting season is cool and rainy. Bean seed, for instance, rots easily if the ground is too cool and wet. The only solution is to replant.

thinning

The technique of knowing how thickly to plant seed develops with experience. First-year gardeners almost always sow too thickly. Once the seedlings do appear they grow rapidly, and when they are large enough to handle, thinning is important. Otherwise, none of the seedlings will have room enough to develop and the results will be spindly, with no worthwhile crops to harvest.

Thinning is a hands-and-knees operation. There is no other way to accomplish it. It must be done as close to

When seedlings come up thickly, they must be thinned so crop has space to grow.

68

the soil and carefully as possible or you run the risk of pulling up the whole row of plants.

New gardeners often find thinning difficult to do. They cringe at the thought of pulling up any young plants. Just remember—it's good for them! And when the little vegetables are about 3 inches high, they are big enough to thin.

Musts for thinning are leaf lettuce, radishes, beets, carrots, turnips, and spinach. Simply go down the row and push aside the young plants to see how thickly the young stems are clumped in the soil, then thin so there is a good finger space between plants. Many little seedlings will come up when this chore is done. Most of them can be used for salads, and are quite tasty if washed thoroughly to get out all the gritty soil particles.

After pulling up the tiny seedlings, press the others remaining in the row gently into the soil to be sure their roots are in good contact. Then, as the crop grows, pull every other seedling to allow for even better spacing. The tiny beets, carrots, and young lettuce plants from this second thinning are especially succulent.

buying transplants

For those who do not have the space or time to spend on starting their own vegetable plants indoors, many garden centers have, each season, an increasing supply of young vegetable transplants with a wider selection of varieties.

There is an art to buying transplants. Those that look the largest and tallest are not necessarily the best buys, and tomato plants already in flower may not be the ones to choose; they may be too tall and spindly. The better choices are the younger, stronger plants that have grown along at a steady rate and have not been pushed too fast. They grab hold more quickly when set out.

Look for transplants that are strong stemmed and of a good green color. Feel the foliage to be sure it is turgid and strong. Most transplants are grown by large wholesale growers and shipped to the various retail centers in spring. If the garden center is adept at caring for these plants, they should hold up well.

But too often transplants find their way to quick-sale discount centers, where they are given casual care— usually too much watering or a baking in hot sun all day—and they deteriorate rapidly. You will find your best buys at quality garden centers where the staff knows how to care for the plants and can guide your choice.

Also, examine boxes of transplants carefully. You might just be buying troubles along with the purchase price. These troubles could be whitefly, especially on tomato plants, and mealybug on peppers or eggplant. Look over transplants carefully, under the leaves and at the stem axils. Reject any weak and spindly yellow-leaved transplants, even if they are half price. If it's not the end of the season, there is probably good reason why the seedlings are offered for quick sale.

setting out transplants

Before any transplants can be set outdoors, they should be hardened off. Those bought commercially, however, have usually been outdoors on the sales benches, and do not need this adjustment. Remember—most transplants require warm weather for planting out, as they are sensitive to cold weather, so wait until the weather is settled. And be sure they are watered well before they are planted.

Setting out the young vegetable plants is quite simple to do. It is usually one of the last planting chores, and when the little plants are all lined up in place in their rows, the garden usually looks quite professional.

The tools needed for transplanting are trowel and watering can. Some gardeners like to set their tomato stakes in place first, before setting out the tomato plants, but they can be placed afterwards. Either way is fine.

To plant transplants, dig a generous hole with the trowel, deep enough to set the little seedling slightly deeper than the top of the peat pot. This will give the plant good depth and support and also assure that the peat pot is completely underground so it decomposes well. Wetting the peat pot well before setting out the plant will assure its beginning to decompose. If the transplant is growing in one of the cylinders covered with plastic netting, cut or pull off the netting, as the roots do not always grow strong enough to break it.

Once the transplant is set in the hole, push the soil around it and gently firm it with your hands. Then water. This watering soaks in all around the air spaces, filling any open air pockets and settling the plant into the soil.

Set tomato seedlings deep enough so that the peat pot is completely covered. Water thoroughly after setting outdoors.

Water with plain water or a starter solution, made from water-soluble fertilizer, such as fish emulsion at half rate, or manure tea. Manure tea is made by soaking a cheesecloth bag of manure, either dried or fresh, in a tub of water for several days until it is the color of dark tea. Dilute it to the color of iced tea and use as a starter solution for the transplants.

For setting out transplants in black plastic mulch, see the chapter on mulching.

caution

Transplants have enemies—cutworms and slugs. Where they have been a problem in the past, be wary and take precautions against them.

Cutworms are the gray-white caterpillars of night-flying moths. They live under the soil, coiled up. (If you see them when preparing the soil, kill them.) They come near the surface at night, cut off the succulent stems of the transplants, and nibble on the knocked-down foliage.

To foil these night raiders, place a paper collar around each transplant when it is set out. Be sure that it extends 2 to 3 inches down into the soil as well as above to protect the young stem. One of the best collars is a section of a quart milk carton, open at top and bottom. Start saving milk cartons in early spring to have a large enough supply. The collar can be pulled out of the soil when the stems have grown thick enough to resist cutworms.

Slugs, also night raiders, live on the surface of the soil and feed on leaves at night. They are mollusks, snails without shells. To keep them away from transplants, spread a thick layer of wood ash or sand on the surface of the soil around the transplant. They dislike crawling over it. Or place shallow pie tins of beer out at dusk. The slugs will crawl in and drown. Empty the tin in the morning and refill. Continue for several evenings.

caring

Once the planting is completed, the garden is well on its way. The biggest tasks ahead are weed control, watering, and watching, either for supplemental fertilizer needs or pest controls.

Mulches are the best means of weed control (see the chapter on mulching); they also preserve moisture and

73

keep the soil cool. If mulching is not possible, then the next best measure for weed control is frequent light hoeing to keep weeds down and the soil airy to receive rainfall. If weeds are not kept down they will take over, as they are more aggressive growers.

The best hoe is a scuffle hoe. Placed flat on the ground, it is then pushed along the soil. It cannot dig deeply to break off shallow roots, yet it is perfect to decapitate weeds at their necks. This type of hoe requires very little effort. Others may prefer the standard garden hoe, but it should be used lightly, to avoid cutting off plant roots that are just at the surface.

As the vegetable garden grows along, a side dressing of fertilizer—a pencil-thin tracing of fertilizer along the row—may be needed. Rake the fertilizer in lightly and apply ideally just before rain. Two important times to apply a supplementary feeding are when flowers are forming on tomatoes, peppers, eggplants, melons, and squash and when the root crops are just beginning to form good, mature roots.

vegetables to grow

artichoke

(Cynara scolymus)

The artichoke, a native of the
Mediterranean region, is closely
related to the cardoon, once
popular in ancient Greece and
Rome. It is not an easy garden
plant to grow, but for those who
insist, it is included.

where to grow Artichokes need a long, frost-free growing season with damp, foggy weather. They are raised commercially along California's coast, from San Francisco southward, and in the coastal regions of Louisiana.

variety Green Globe.

soil The artichoke is a perennial requiring plenty of room to spread, so the soil should be well drained and reasonably fertile.

planting In artichoke-growing regions, the root divisions are sold for planting and set out, 4 feet apart, in late winter or early spring. Set them so the succulent base, which gives rise to the new shoots, is just at soil level or slightly above. The woody root stem should extend straight down, deep into the soil.

how it grows The artichoke is an enormous plant—it may grow over 6 feet tall and spread almost as wide—and resembles a thistle with rather attractive foliage. The part of the plant that is eaten is the unopened flower head, which has a fleshy calyx base. The flower receptacle or artichoke heart is the most delectable portion. There may be just a few artichokes to cut the first year, with full harvest in the second.

culture Keep weeds out of the artichoke patch with frequent cultivation or heavy mulching. The plants should be well watered during any dry spells, especially the first year. Fertilizer with a high nitrogen content is applied just as the tiny buds are beginning to form, and again at the end of the harvest. When the last artichoke bud is cut from each branch, the plant gradually yellows. Cut stems to the ground. New shoots will grow in spring for the next season's crop.

harvest The unripened flower heads must be cut before the bracts start to separate. Usually they are about 3 to 4 inches long. The main terminal bud of each stalk is preferred, but the smaller buds of the side shoots are just as tasty.

pests None of major importance.

diseases None.

asparagus
(Asparagus officinalis)

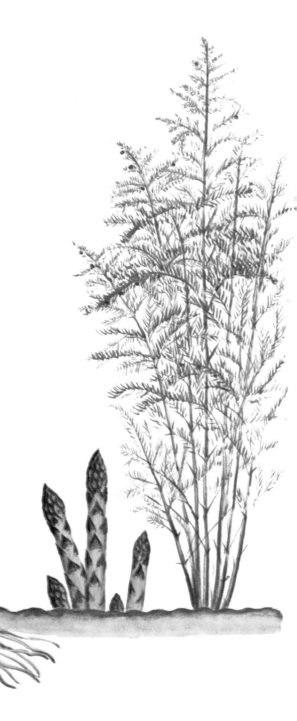

A perennial, the asparagus belongs to the lily family, and can be found growing wild on the shorelines and river banks in many parts of Europe, and on the steppes of Russia. Both the Greeks and Romans enjoyed this succulent vegetable, and transplanted the young wild plants to their cultivated plots. The early American colonists enjoyed asparagus boiled and flavored with "butter, vinegar, and pepper, oyl and vinegar, or as every one's manner doth please." The house plants called "asparagus ferns" are closely related to this vegetable, whose top growth in summer resembles a feathery fern.

where to grow   A perennial vegetable that thrives almost anywhere in the continental United States except where summers are long and humid. Proper soil preparation before planting and good summer maintenance will keep this vegetable yielding for a minimum of 10 years, and possibly as long as 15 or more. Because it takes up permanent garden space, it should be given a specially designated spot. It is often planted near rhubarb, another long-lived garden perennial.

varieties   Mary Washington (rust resistant); Waltham Washington (rust resistant).

soil   The best soil is a sandy, well-drained loam heavily enriched with well-rotted manure and compost. Ground prepared in this way dries out quickly in early spring, to spur the early growth of the spears. pH should be 6.5. Average garden soil, however, will support a good asparagus crop, provided it drains well. Rocky New England soil hampers the development of straight spears. Ideally, the soil should be prepared to a depth of 1 foot, a week to 10 days before planting, adding the rotted manure and compost and working it in well. Fertilizer application: 4 pounds of 5-10-10 per 100 square feet, or generous quantities of bone meal or ground phosphate rock and wood ash.

planting   *When:* As soon as the ground can be worked.

How: Slow way: Start with seed, which requires 1 month to germinate. To hasten germination a bit, soak the seed for 2 days in water. Plant seeds ½ inch deep in rows 2 feet wide, thin seedlings to 3 to 4 inches between plants. These seedlings should grow for a summer, and the following year the "yearlings" should be transplanted to the permanent asparagus bed.

Fast way: Buy year-old plants, or "crowns," from seedsmen. They will have tight compact buds with masses of supple dangling roots. Plants are set out in trenches, dug to a depth of 6 to 8 inches and spaced 4 feet apart, in the prepared soil bed. Mound the soil to the side of each trench, as it will be used to backfill as the asparagus grow. Set the asparagus crowns in the base of the trench, with 18 inches between plants, and cover with about 2 inches of soil. As the asparagus tips grow during the summer, the trenches will be filled in gradually, until they are completely filled by the end of the summer. Asparagus plants have a tendency to "rise" as they grow mature, hence the need for the trenching method of planting.

how it grows   The roots will spread horizontally rather than down, and in years to come will produce a thick mat of roots and underground shoots. The first year after planting the spears will be spindly and thin. As they mature they develop into tall, ferny branchlets, quite lovely to see. The true asparagus leaves have been reduced to the triangular scales on the spears, which are cut off when the asparagus is cleaned for cooking.

The plant is dioecious, having tiny male and female flowers and a small berry for a fruit. There has been some thought that the male plants produce more spears, but this has not been confirmed. The ferny top growth is actually producing food for the shoots below in much the same manner as bulb foliage renews a bulb underground for next spring's flower. For this reason, asparagus foliage should not be cut down too soon, but should be allowed to wither off naturally. It can be cut down and left as mulch or left standing.

culture Weeds are the biggest problem with asparagus since they offer too much competition for the developing shoots, and an untidy asparagus patch can develop very quickly. Frequent light, shallow cultivation is a good preventive. Light mulching is another. First cultivation should be in early spring, before the spears appear above ground. At this time, lightly apply fertilizer, preferably well-rotted manure or ½ ounce of nitrate of soda, to each plant, and continue cultivation until the tops have grown too high and thick to manage with a shallow scuffle hoe. Also, watering is extremely important any time there is lack of adequate rainfall during the growing season. When harvesting has been completed, feed the asparagus bed with a well-balanced fertilizer to encourage a generous crop of succulent spears the next spring.

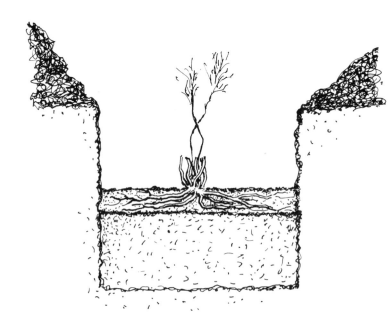

harvest The succulent tenderness of asparagus depends on the quality of the soil, the rapidity of shoot development in spring, and adequate soil moisture. No harvesting will occur the first year plants are set out, a few spears may be cut the second year, and full harvest will be available the third year. At full harvest year, cutting may last for 4 to 6 weeks, depending on the growing season and how well the asparagus plantings have been managed. At the beginning of the harvest period, spears may be ready 2 or 3 times a week. They are tastiest when just about 6 inches tall and tight at the tip, not spreading. At the height of the growing season there may be fresh spears to select each day. Harvest stops when the spears begin to look thin and spindly. Stop cutting when hot summer weather comes.

There are two schools of thought on cutting. One is to cut the spears off with a sharp knife (asparagus knife preferably) just at ground level to avoid damaging any roots underground. A simpler method is to snap the spears off at ground level.

Asparagus is similar to corn in that quality deteriorates soon after picking. For best flavor, pick it just before it is to be cooked. If this can't be done, then refrigerate it promptly.

pests *Asparagus beetle:* Handpick.

diseases Rust has been virtually eliminated by the development of rust-resistant varieties.

beans

(Phaseolus sp.)

The botanical name Phaseolus is derived
from the Greek *fasiolos* and the Roman
phasiolus, which suggests that this world-
wide source of food has been grown
since ancient times. The Indians of the
New World grew the bean long before
the Pilgrims landed. John Verrazano
referred to them in 1524. Even earlier,
Columbus found a "sort of bean" growing
in Cuba, "very different from those
of Spain." Explorers took seeds of these
beans back to Europe, where they gained
popularity. They were returned to the
New World by various settlers in
much improved forms. Lima beans
(P. lunatus) take their name from Lima,
Peru, where they were found in ancient
tombs. The name "string bean" once
referred to a bean with fibrous strings
that joined the pods together and had to
be pulled off before eating. This variety
was eliminated with the introduction
of the Stringless Green Pod in 1896. The
term "snap bean" is now used, and they
are either wax or green.

where to grow Beans can be grown in average soil, almost anywhere in the United States. They grow best if the soil is well drained and the summer is consistently warm. Seed will rot in the ground in cold, damp weather. Since beans are subject to downy mildew, they should not be grown where there are cold summer fogs.

varieties *Bush:* Tendercrop; Top Crop; Burpee's Tenderpod; Provider.

Bush wax: Eastern Butter Wax; Burpee's Brittle Wax; Pencil Pod Wax.

Pole: Kentucky Wonder; Blue Lake; Scarlet Runner.

Lima: Fordhook 242; Henderson.

Pole lima: King of the Garden.

Other beans: Bush or pole Romano, Italian broad bean; French Horticultural, long yellow pods mottled red; Long Pod, broad or fava bean.

soil Warm soil is essential, especially for limas. pH range between 6 and 7, just slightly acid. Bush beans will thrive in fertile loam soil without addition of fertilizer. Too much fertilizer will promote foliage growth and little crop. Limas and pole beans are heavy feeders. Legume inoculant is available from seed suppliers for seed treatment, especially if beans or peas have not been grown in the soil before.

planting *When:* After the soil is sufficiently warm—temperatures above 75 degrees. Beans are easily killed by frost.

How: Bush: Germination in 7 days. Plant seeds 2 inches apart, 1 to 1½ inches deep in rows 2 feet apart. Thin to about 6 to 8 plants per foot of row.
  Bean plants produce the bulk of their crop for a 2-week period. Rather than plant the entire row, sections should be planted at 2-week intervals until mid-July, or 8 weeks before the first killing frost. This will assure a steady crop all summer. Harvest: Average 50 days.
Wax, Limas: Germination in 10 days. Plant seeds 3 to 4 inches apart, with eyes down, 1 inch deep in rows 2 feet apart. Two plantings a month apart produce a prolonged harvest. Harvest: Average 65–75 days.
Pole: Germination in 8 to 14 days. Set 3 rough-barked, 6-foot poles in the ground, tepee fashion, and tie together at the top. Leave 3 to 4 feet between pole groups. Make a hill at the base of each pole, enriched with compost or well-rotted manure, and plant 6 to 8 seeds in each. After the second pair of true leaves appears, thin to 3 plants per pole. With regular harvesting, the pole beans should bear all summer. Harvest: 65 days.

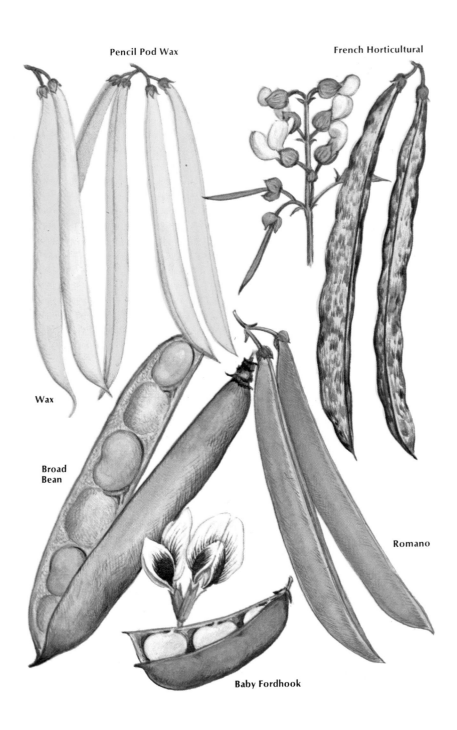

Pencil Pod Wax

French Horticultural

Wax

Broad
Bean

Romano

Baby Fordhook

culture Keep rows weed free with shallow cultivation or heavy mulching; beans are shallow rooted, and should not be cultivated deeply. Never work around beans after a rainfall or in the early morning when the leaves are still wet from dew. The plants are susceptible to rust, which spreads when the foliage is wet. Water weekly and deeply during dry spells, as beans need constant soil moisture to develop properly. Feed pole varieties by working a thin band of 5-10-5 or 4-12-12 around each hill, once at planting time and again as beans start to form.

harvest Watch plants carefully as beans start to form and harvest every 2 to 3 days. Beans are ready to pick when the pods are well formed and rounded and snap readily if bent in half. Wax beans should have good yellow color. Be sure to lift up the bean plants and look under the foliage to pick every ripe bean. This will promote a continued crop. If beans are left on the plants too long, the seeds overdevelop and the pods become tough. Poorly formed pods are caused by too dry soil, poor unfertile soil, or insect damage. Limas are picked when the pods are well filled and still green in color. If the pods are yellowing, the beans are too mature and can be left on the vine and picked later to use as dry beans.

pests *Mexican bean beetle:* A coppery brown beetle with black spots that lays yellow eggs and goes through an ugly nymph (immature) stage. Crush the yellow egg clusters when seen and hand pick beetles. Use rotenone or pyrethrum. Plant marigolds between rows to repel beetles.

Aphids: Rotenone. Plant nasturtiums between rows.

Seed corn maggots: Spray diazinon in the furrow when planting.

diseases Bean seed is often pretreated before sale with Captan, a fungicide that protects seed for germination in wet weather.

Anthracnose: Clean up after crop is harvested. Never work around wet beans. Buy quality seed.

Bacterial blight: Same as for anthracnose.

Mosaic: Grow resistant varieties.

Downy mildew: Do not grow in foggy regions.

beet

(Beta vulgaris)

The beet, or beetroot as it is known in
Europe, is a relatively modern vegetable, for
it was not until the sixteenth century
that it became popular for its root. Prior
to this time the Greeks, Romans, and
Europeans of the Middle Ages grew leaf beet,
or what is now known as Swiss chard *(Beta
vulgaris cicla).* Commercial agriculture makes
use of the beet in many forms—the
mangel-wurzel or mangel used for cattle
feed and the sugar beet for sugar.

where to grow   Beets thrive in all parts of the country.

varieties   Detroit Dark Red; Early Wonder; Ruby Queen; Firechief; Burpee's Golden, an unusual beet with sweet golden flesh that does not bleed when cooked; Long Season, a slow-growing long beet, roughly shaped and harvested in early fall or for winter storage.

soil   Beets grow in average garden soil. The best crop is achieved with pH 6.5 in a rich, sandy loam prepared with well-rotted manure and compost to a depth of 8 inches. Beets do not thrive if pH is below 6. The soil should be well pulverized to remove stones and clods so that roots form well and rapidly.

planting   Germination in 7 days.

When: Beets are hardy and may be sown as soon as the ground can be worked. For succession crop, plantings can be made every 2 weeks to midsummer. Beets become tough and stringy if grown in hot weather during droughts; ample water supply is essential to succulent roots. A late summer crop can be sown for fall harvest.

How: Sow seed ½ inch deep in rows 12 to 18 inches apart. The beet seed is a compact ball of many tiny seeds. Many plants germinate where each seed is sown, so seed should be placed sparingly. When seedlings are 4 to 6 inches high, thin plants to stand 1½ inches apart. (The thinnings can be used in salad or cooked as spinach.) Then, as these beets grow to about an inch in diameter, pull every other one to allow larger beets to grow.

how it grows   The beet develops a red-colored, semiglobe-shaped root with succulent tops that may be cooked as a spinach substitute. Because the seed is a compact seed, unless the plants are thinned properly, they will not develop into nicely rounded roots. "White rings" that occur in the beets are the result of poor growing climate—drought or alternate heavy rains and drought.

culture   The rows should be cultivated shallowly halfway through growth period to keep weeds down, or the rows may be heavily mulched to keep them weed free.

harvest   60 days. The roots are best when 1½ to 3 inches in diameter. They deteriorate if left in the ground much longer than 10 days after reaching full size.

pests   None of major concern.

diseases   None of major concern.

broccoli
(Brassica oleracea italica)

Linnaeus, the father of botany, believed broccoli and cauliflower were so similar that he grouped them together. The English horticulturists of the eighteenth century were not much clearer in their thinking, as they referred to broccoli as "sprout colli-flower." Evidently, however, the Italian gourmets realized the difference between the two, and our modern broccoli comes from them. Technically the plants are quite similar, but broccoli "sprouts" and cauliflower "heads."

where to grow   A cool-season crop, broccoli does best where it has cool weather (spring or fall) to mature.

varieties   Italian Green Sprouting (spring); Waltham 29 (fall); Green Comet; Raaba, a branching, nonheading variety.

soil   Average garden soil, well drained.

planting   Germination in 7 days.

When: Start seed indoors 6 weeks before the last killing frost, for early spring crop. (In midsummer, start another crop of seedlings for August planting and late fall crop.) Set out seedlings in late April, early May. Broccoli is hardier than cauliflower, and can withstand several frosts and still keep producing.

How: In rows 2½ feet apart, with 18 inches to 2 feet between plants.

how it grows   The plant grows relatively erect, to 4 feet tall, with long, narrow, deep green leaves. As the harvest nears, a thickened cluster appears at the top of the stalk, which is actually a flower head. When it is cut off for harvest, side shoots will continue to develop for several weeks.

culture   Since the plants are shallow rooted, cultivation to keep down weeds should be careful and shallow, or mulch rows heavily to keep down weeds and conserve soil moisture. Once growth begins, the plants need continually moist soil. Watering will be important whenever rainfall is scant. Just as the first crop is developing, apply a ring of fertilizer 5-10-5 or 4-8-4 around each plant, 6 inches from the stem, and scratch in about 1 tablespoonful per plant. Or water with water-soluble fish emulsion fertilizer.

harvest   60–80 days from plants. The first crop will be the central flower head, which resembles a green cauliflower; cut it off with a sharp knife to a 4- to 6-inch stem. Be sure the head is cut before it cracks apart and separates; otherwise the plant will go quickly to seed. When the terminal flower head is cut off, smaller side shoots will develop a continual harvest.

pests   Same as for cabbage.

diseases   Same as for cabbage.

brussels sprouts

(Brassica oleracea gemmifera)

The vegetable is named for
Brussels, Belgium, which was
the center of a sprout-
growing region. The
vegetable is of fairly recent
introduction, since it was
little known outside Belgium
and France until the mid-
nineteenth century. It is a
very popular vegetable in
England.

where to grow Brussels sprouts are a cool-season vegetable, and should not be grown where the summers are long, hot, and dry.

varieties Jade Cross; Long Island Improved.

soil Average garden soil enriched with compost and rotted manure, the same type of soil that will support all members of the cabbage family.

planting Germination in 4–10 days.

When: Start seed indoors in early May so plants are ready to set out in June or early July. The sprouts develop best in cool weather.

How: In rows 3 feet apart, with 30 inches between plants.

how it grows This is one of the strangest looking vegetables. The plant produces tiny little cabbage heads in the axils of the leaves along a strong central stalk. As the sprouts develop the leaves are broken off, so that eventually what appears is a fat, upright stem covered with clusters of sprouts and topped with long green leaves, much like a shortened palm tree. Sprouts develop from the bottom of the plant upward.

culture Keep weed free with shallow cultivation or heavy mulching. Grow in the same manner as all cabbage family plants. As soon as the lower sprouts begin to mature, pinch out the growing shoot at the top of each plant (not the entire leaf top). This will stop the top from growing and encourage the sprouts to ripen along the stalk.

harvest 3 months. When sprouts first appear, the lower leaf should be cut off. The sprouts should be picked green when about an inch or so in diameter. To pick them, twist them off. Each plant should yield about 1 quart of sprouts. Harvest continues well into the cold fall months. Light snow does not seem to stop their developing, and even improves their flavor. The Burpee Seed Company reported a harvest of frozen sprouts from field plants in January. Some gardeners in severely cold winter climates may prefer to dig plants still loaded with sprouts and keep them in a cool, light place, where they will continue to ripen.

pests Same as for cabbage.

diseases Same as for cabbage.

cabbage
(Brassica oleracea capitata)

Cabbage is the "father" of the whole
mustard family or Brassica, which includes
mustard, broccoli, cauliflower, kale, collards,
turnips, and kohlrabi. Cultivated forms
known today are believed to have stemmed
from the original wild cabbages found on
the white cliffs of Dover and in the coastal
regions of Denmark and northwestern
France. In spite of its widespread habitat,
cabbage was not actually cultivated in
England until the mid-nineteenth century.
Cromwell's troops introduced cabbage to
Scotland, and the French explorer Jacques
Cartier introduced it to Canada. By 1669 it
was growing in Virginia.

where to grow Practically a national vegetable, cabbage grows best where there is a cool, moist growing season.

varieties There are many types of cabbages: green, red, savoy (with crinkled leaves), and Chinese (see separate entry). For an extended harvest, gardeners usually choose early, midseason, and late varieties to ripen through the growing season, with some space left in the garden for the unusual red and Chinese varieties.

Early: Golden Acre (yellows resistant); Stonehead Hybrid (yellows resistant); Market Prize; Early Jersey Wakefield.

Midsummer: Greenback; Copenhagen Market; King Cole.

Late or winter: Danish Ballhead.

Savoy: Vanguard; Savoy King.

Red: Ruby Ball; Red Acre; Mammoth Red Rock.

Miniature: Dwarf Morden.

soil Cabbages are heavy feeders all during their long growing season and need fertile, well-drained soil deeply enriched with compost and a high-nitrogen–potassium fertilizer such as 5-10-10 (1 pound per square foot) or generous quantities of blood meal, cottonseed meal, and ground rock phosphate. Cabbage needs abundant soil moisture to develop properly. Watering is important during any summer dry spells.

planting Germination in 5 to 7 days.

When: Start seed indoors in early February for setting out when ground is workable for July harvest; in mid-March for setting out May 1 for August harvest; and in mid-May for setting out in early July for October harvest. Adjustments can be made in this schedule depending on local climate.

How: In rows 2½ feet apart, with 12–16 inches between plants. For late varieties, rows 3 feet apart and plants 2 feet apart.
  One of the drawbacks in growing members of the mustard family is their susceptibility to many insect pests and soil-borne diseases. A general good gardening practice to follow is crop rotation. Never grow cabbage or any other Brassica in the same soil year after year. Allow at least a 3-year interval.

how it grows Cabbage is a wide-spreading foliage plant with handsome leaves that form a tight, hard ball head on a strong central stem.

culture For best results, the cabbage must be kept well fed and watered during the entire growing season. In dry weather the heads form too soon, and with irregular growing conditions they may crack apart. Cabbages are shallow rooted, and difficult to cultivate with-

Red

Savoy

out snapping some of the shallow feeder roots. Mulches work best to keep weeds out. Feed with a high N-K fertilizer when seedlings are set out, again in three weeks, and again when heads first start to form. Side dress by tracing a thin line of fertilizer along the row about 4 inches from the plants, scratch in lightly, and water (unless rain is imminent). Water-soluble fish emulsion may also be used.

harvest 3–4 months. Cabbage heads must feel hard and solid before cutting. When harvesting, use a sharp knife to cut the head off at the base of the plant, keeping a few outer leaves to protect the head. The heads must be harvested promptly, or they deteriorate in the field. If there is ample cool, dry storage space, the heads may be harvested and stored for use. Or the ripe heads can be stored in the field by stopping plant growth. To do this, pull the plant up slightly from the ground until a few roots can be heard snapping. This will hold the plant for a short period until it can be picked. Some European gardeners have reported success in storing cabbage plants by burying them upside down in a deep soil pit with a thin straw flooring and covering them completely with soil to just below frost line, with another straw mulch on top.

pests *Root maggot:* Use a ground spray or granules of diazinon at planting time; or place 3-inch tar paper squares around each seedling when transplanting to cover the soil areas; or keep the ground dusted with wood ash.

Cabbage butterflies/worms: Use the new biological control BT *(Bacillus thuringiensis)* or dust with rotenone.

Aphids: Spray with rotenone or pyrethrum.

Cutworms: Use stiff paper collars around transplants to extend at least an inch below soil line.

Flea beetles: Wood ash or flour dust; spray with rotenone.

diseases Soil fungicides are somewhat effective on cabbage diseases, but they are expensive, sold in large quantity, and not practical for small home garden use unless a great deal of cabbage is grown.

Club root fungus: Most frequent in soggy soil or in acid soil. Grow only in well-drained soil; follow crop rotation practices; lime to keep soil pH at neutral (7).

Yellows: A soil-borne disease; choose resistant varieties.

Black rot: Bacteria borne on seed; buy only from reputable seed dealers or bedding plant growers. Rotate crops.

Blackleg: Bacteria spreads from infected plants, garden tools, and leftover debris. Follow crop rotation.

carrot

(Daucus carota sativa)

Thanks to the efforts of a well-known French
horticulturist, Vilmorin-Andrieux, the carrot as we
know it today came into being. More than 100 years
ago, working with the common wild flower Queen
Anne's lace, he cultivated and selected plants over
a 3- to 4-year period finally producing a thick, bright
orange root on the plant. The carrot, widely popular
in Europe and America, is highly favored for its
crispness, flavor, and high vitamin A content.

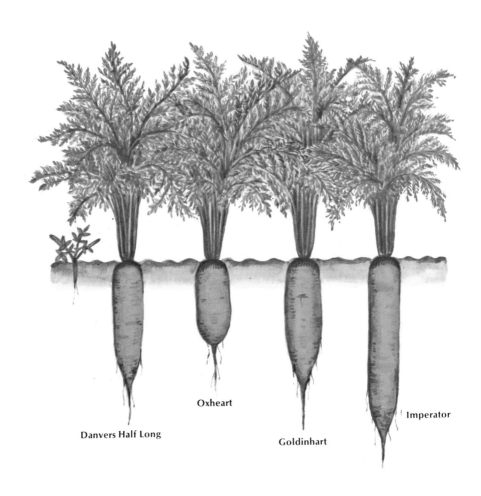

Oxheart

Imperator

Danvers Half Long

Goldinhart

where to grow   Practically everywhere.

varieties   Carrot varieties are short, medium, and long. Variety selection should be determined by the kind of soil in which they will be grown: tight clay soils for the short carrots; rich, loamy, well-drained soils for the longest kinds. In order of root length: Oxheart (4½ inches); Royal Chantenay; Danvers Half Long or Danvers 126; Goldinhart (5½–7 inches); Scarlet Nantes; Pioneer (7 inches); Gold Pak; Tendersweet; Imperator (8–9 inches).

soil   pH 6–6.5 is best. Proper soil is the key to success with carrots. Ideally it should be very fertile, deep, and easily worked, with ample quantities of humus to permit the roots to grow quickly and straight. The more natural fertility in the soil, the sweeter the carrot. Heavy clay soils do not support good carrot growth.

planting   Germination in 10 days to 3 weeks.

When: Carrots are hardy, and can be planted as soon as the ground can be worked. For a continual crop, sections of the row can be planted every 2 weeks to late May. For a fall crop, more sowings can be started in late July.

How: Since carrot seed germinates slowly, it can be mixed with radish or leaf lettuce, which germinate quickly and mark the row. (The pulling of radish and leaf lettuce plants will also provide some natural thinning.) Or the seed can be mixed with sand or dry compost to make sowing easier. Space rows a foot apart, and thin seedlings to 2 inches spacing when about 3 inches high. Pull every other carrot to allow more spacing as carrots mature.

culture   Carrots grow slowly, at first sending down a tiny orange root that expands and develops more quickly toward the end of its growing period. As with all root crops, rapid, steady development produces the best results. Keep the row weed free with light shallow cultivation or heavy mulching. The seedlings must have steady moisture to develop well, with less moisture as the roots mature. Too much moisture at the end of the maturing period may cause the roots to crack.

harvest   Mature carrots will be ready in about 2 months, although some gardeners find them more succulent when they are pulled younger. A tiny head or crown of orange will appear at the soil line when the carrots are maturing. Pull only those carrots needed since they remain fresh in the ground for some time. The late summer crop can be harvested in winter if mulched.

pests   None of major concern.

diseases   None of major concern.

cauliflower

(Brassica oleracea botrytis)

Originally from the
Mediterranean region,
particularly Cyprus, cauliflower and its very close
relative broccoli have similar
culture. If gardeners have
to eliminate a crop because
of space limitations, this
may be the one. Cauliflower,
being so much dependent
on proper weather, is finicky
to grow. It languishes if
the weather turns suddenly
hot, or bolts to small button
heads rather than one
compact head. If it is rainy
when the heads are
maturing and blanching,
they may rot. The crop is
grown commercially in the
more favorable market
basket climate of California.

where to grow Wherever there are steady, cool growing seasons, frost free.

varieties Early Snowball; Snowball Imperial; Self-Blanch (fall); and Early Purple-Head (fall, not blanched).

soil Fertile, enriched loam is ideal with pH 6 to 7. Cauliflower is sensitive to boron deficiency in the soil.

planting Germination 3–10 days.

When: Start seed indoors 6 weeks before the last killing frost. The plants are not as cold hardy as other members of the cabbage family, so they should be set out in April. For fall crop, start seed in mid-June to set out transplants in late July. Allow 2 to 3 months' growing time before first frost.

How: In rows 2½–3 feet apart, with 2 feet between plants.

how it grows The plant has broad green-blue foliage that develops a central flower head. This increases in size to a large, cabbage-sized head of condensed flowers. By tradition the head is blanched (covered from the sun) to bleach it white.

culture The trick to cauliflower is to keep it growing steadily once the seedlings are planted outdoors. So much, however, does depend on proper growing weather—ideally, a cool, long, sunny season with ample moisture or irrigation. When the center begins to develop a tight flower head about the size of a McIntosh apple, loosely tie the outer leaves with twine. Do not tie too tightly, as there must be some air circulation. This will cause the flower head to bleach white in about 1 to 2 weeks.

harvest 60–80 days, from plants. As soon as the compact head is formed and blanched, it should be cut off with a sharp knife, along with several of the leaves for protection. If too many heads ripen at once, cut them anyway and store in a cool, dark place for several weeks. Ripened heads left on the plant will rot and deteriorate rapidly.

pests Same as for cabbage.

diseases Same as for cabbage.

celeriac

(Apium graveolens rapaceum)

This odd form of celery is grown for
its swollen root, which develops
just at ground level. Unlike celery, the
dark green stems are hollow and the
foliage is a beautiful, deep green.
The plant is best known among the
French and Germans, who use it in
stews or eat it raw, grated, or sliced
in salads. Sometimes it is called "turnip-
rooted celery."

where to grow	Where there is a steady, rather cool growing season for at least four months. It is not suited to hot drought summers.
variety	Alabaster.
soil	Same as for celery.
planting	Germination in 2–3 weeks.
	When: Start seed indoors at least 6 to 7 weeks before planting outdoors in early spring. A second crop is sometimes grown by seeding directly outdoors in spring.
	How: In rows 2 feet apart, with 4–6 inches between plants.
how it grows	Celeriac is a hollow-stemmed celery that produces a thick root. The root, which has a flavor suggesting parsley and celery, is edible; the leaves are not.
culture	The plant needs two essentials to develop: constant soil moisture and weed-free soil. Whenever rainfall is scant, watering is important. Since the soil is made fertile at planting time, the only additional feeding is usually 2 weeks after seedlings are set out or 10 days or so after the seedlings (directly sown) are thinned.
harvest	4 months. There are two schools of thought on harvesting. Some growers merely pull up the plant and cut off the top when the swollen root is about 3 to 4 inches wide. Others watch the tuber's development, and when it is beginning to form, they gradually snip off the side roots and hill soil up over the swollen root area for a short period of time to partially blanch it. Both systems might be tried to determine the best for the local soil and climate.
pests	Same as for celery.
diseases	Same as for celery.

celery

(Apium graveolens dulce)

Smallage, a plant found in marshy ground throughout northern Europe, may have been modern celery's ancestor, although some believe it to be the selinon (or parsley) mentioned in the *Odyssey* of Homer. To the ancients, the plant had more medicinal than culinary importance, a fact based upon ninth-century French writings. Not until the seventeenth and eighteenth centuries did the merits of celery as a vegetable gain any recognition. The Swedes led the way by using stored celery during the winter months. The old custom of blanching the plants to make them white is not practiced much today, as the newer varieties have excellent flavor when green.

where to grow   Where there is a long, steady, cool growing season of about 4 months and no hot, dry summers.

varieties   Golden Self-blanching; Summer Pascal; Utah 52-70.

soil   More than climate, the soil quality will determine whether it is practical to grow celery. Farmers used to consider river-bottom muck soils "celery soil." And that is what celery needs—highly fertile soil well enriched with compost, well-rotted manure, and peat moss. The crop needs moisture constantly, as well as high quantities of nutrients for fast growth.

planting   Germination in 2–3 weeks.

When: Celery seed is usually started indoors about 10 weeks before it is time to set the plants outdoors—that is, after the soil is warm and the air temperature settled. The seed is minute and finicky, and is started in much the same manner as African violet seed, in closed containers to keep seedlings moist. A simpler method is to buy transplants. Some gardeners who have a long frost-free autumn season can seed a late winter crop directly.

How: In rows 2 feet apart; with 6–8 inches between plants.

how it grows   Celery is a biennial that, if left for its second year, would produce flowers and seed. It is harvested when immature.

culture   When seedlings are set out they need a quick start, which is usually provided by watering the plants with a water-soluble high-nitrogen fertilizer. Since the plants have fine, almost hair-like roots, use a heavy mulch to keep down weeds.

Blanching: Few gardeners blanch (or bleach white) celery. For those who want to experiment, select a few plants then wrap them from top to bottom with heavy paper, perhaps a super-market bag cut to shape, and tied loosely with string. Only the top leaves should be allowed to show. Blanching should be done about 2 weeks before harvest.

harvest   3 months after transplants are set out; 4 months from seed. Cut plants at the base, just beneath the crown, with a sharp knife and remove some of the outer leaves. Celery will easily keep for several weeks if stored in a cool, dark place.

pests   *Celery leaf tier:* Pyrethrum or rotenone dust.

Celery worm (larvae of the black swallowtail butterfly): Hand pick.

diseases   *Early/late blight:* Buy quality seed and transplants; clean up the garden after each crop is harvested.

chinese cabbage

(Brassica chinensis; B. pekinensis)

There are two forms of what is known as Chinese cabbage: Bok choy *(B. chinensis)*, which grows more like a chard than a cabbage and has oblong, shiny green leaves on swollen white stems; and wong bok *(B. pekinensis)*, which suggests cos lettuce with its long, compact head with crinkled leaves at the outer edges. Both are annuals, and with the interest in Chinese cookery, are becoming increasingly popular. Some gourmets prefer these cabbages for slaw and cooking to the head types.

Bok Choy

Wong Bok

where to grow	A cool-season crop, they grow best where they have a cool fall growing season to develop. Otherwise, they bolt to seed.
varieties	Michihli; Burpee Hybrid; Early Hybrid G (wong bok or celery cabbage); Crispy Choy (bok choy or non-heading cabbage).
soil	Same as for cabbage.
planting	*When:* Plant in midsummer for fall harvest. *How:* Seed should be sown directly in the ground in rows 2½ feet apart; plants thinned to 18 inches apart.
culture	Same as for cabbage.
harvest	2½ to 3 months. When "heads" feel compact and firm, they should be cut off at the ground with a few outer leaves for protection.
pests	Same as for cabbage.
diseases	Same as for cabbage.

collards
(Brassica oleracea acephala)

A warm-weather, nonheading cabbage,
popular in the South and grown for its
crown of smooth, edible, dark blue green
leaves. A variety of kale, that has cut or
deeply curved leaves, collards are often
called "colewort," derived from the Latin
caulis, meaning "stalk." Another name is
"tree cabbage." Collards do not produce
edible flowers like cauliflower and broccoli,
but their leaves are rich in vitamin A and
ascorbic acid. Like kale, collards have been
cultivated since the times of the ancient
Greeks and Romans.

   Collards are so closely related to kale they
have the same botanical name. The easiest
way to tell the difference between the
two is by comparing their growing seasons.
Collards thrive in the summer months; kale
grows best during the cooler late summer–
early fall season.

where to grow Collards can be grown almost anywhere in the United States. Because they withstand summer heat and light frosts, they are cabbage substitutes in warm climates, particularly in the South. Light frosts improve the mild cabbage flavor.

varieties The standard is Georgia; Vates (dwarf type).

soil Average garden soil, but if highly acid, add lime to raise pH to 6.0–6.8.

planting *When:* In warm climates, where the winters are mild, seed is sown in midsummer for late fall–winter harvest. Where winters are severe, seed may be sown in early spring, as soon as the ground can be worked, for a summer harvest, or a month later for early fall harvest.

How: Plant seeds ½ inch deep in rows 3 feet apart, and thin plants to 5–6 inches apart when seedlings are 3 inches tall. Mature plants are 2 to 3 feet tall.

how it grows The plant has an erect stem producing clusters of leaves.

culture Keep the rows weed free with mulching or very shallow cultivation, since collards are shallow rooted. As plants mature, the plant may need a stake support for the top crown.

harvest 70–90 days. When young, whole plants can be cooked. Or, the younger succulent leaves can be cut from the plant like leaf lettuce or Swiss chard to allow more leaves to grow. They may be eaten raw or cooked as cabbage. The whole top may also be cut off and cooked.

pests Same as for cabbage.

diseases Same as for cabbage.

corn

(Zea mays saccharata)

If ever there were a plant that symbolizes America, corn just has to be it. This noble plant was a popular field crop with the North American Indians long before any Europeans ever saw the New World. Columbus was one of the first to take back word of this curious plant, which he found growing in Cuba and again in Venezuela. Corn is truly ancient, with its historic roots in South America. Fossils date it to 2000 B.C., and it is known that the Inca palace gardens were decorated with gold and silver carvings of maize. A type of maize with each grain enclosed in a husk was carried to Central America by the early Peruvians. From Central America the corn found its way to what is now the United States, where the Indians began its cultivation. Their corn was probably a form of field corn used for flour, since our sweet corn did not become a major cultivated crop until a century ago. And only within the last 70 years have the fine, sweet-tasting hybrids come into being.

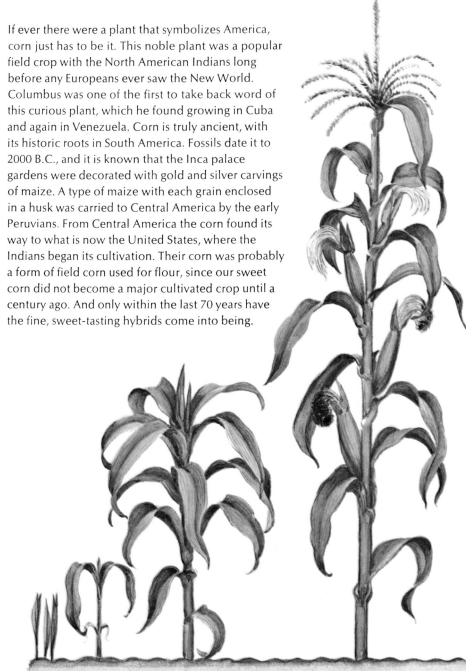

where to grow Corn requires three months of warm, sunny weather to mature, and can grow wherever ample water is available. In cold northern climates with shorter growing seasons (65 days), such as Alaska and northern Canada, dwarf varieties can be grown.

varieties The trick to corn planting is a span of varieties (early, midseason, and late) to spread the harvest over a long season.

Early: Spring Gold; Seneca Explorer.

Midseason: Sundance; Wonderful; Northern Bell; Gold Cup; Golden Cross Bantam.

Late: Seneca Chief; Silver Queen and Country Gentleman Hybrid (white); Sweet Sue; Butter and Sugar; Sugar and Gold (all bi-colors).

Dwarf: White Midget; Golden Midget; Midget Hybrid.

Popcorn: White Cloud; Japanese Hulless.

There also are the ornamental varieties, with colored kernels. These varieties should be grown away from the sweet corn, to avoid any cross pollination.

soil Average garden soil will support a good corn crop, but the best results are obtained when the ground is deeply prepared with well-rotted manure and compost to provide a light, well-draining texture. Corn is a heavy feeder, and needs generous quantities of nutrients, especially phosphorus and potash. Work in one pound of 5-10-10 or 4-8-12 per 25 feet of row, or work bone meal and wood ash into the ground before planting.

planting Germination in 7 to 10 days.

When: The soil must be warm (55–60 degrees) and days and nights warm before corn can be planted, as it is susceptible to frost and cool weather. The easiest way to prolong harvest is to plant early, midseason, and late varieties at the same time. Or if your family has one favorite variety, then plantings can be made every two weeks until 3 months before the first frost.

How: Corn should be planted in a square block area with at least 3 adjacent rows of the same variety, never in one long row, as it is open-wind pollinated and needs neighboring corn plants for good formation of well-filled (pollinated) ears. Gaps in ripe ears are caused by poor pollination. Place rows 3 feet apart. Plant 4 to 5 seeds per foot, 4 inches deep, thinning to 10–12 inches between plants. (Plant dwarf variety seeds 1 inch deep, 30 inches between rows, 8 inches between plants.) Or place corn in hills 3 feet apart, with 4 to 5 seeds per hill, thinned to the 3 strongest plants.

　　If hills are planted, place a scant handful of fertilizer in the bottom of the hill and work it in well before planting the seed. Or

109

Strawberry Popcorn

male

female

follow the Indian advice to the Colonists and work in fish heads and entrails deeply before sowing seed.

how it grows Corn is a monocotyledon, a grasslike plant, as are wheat, oats, lilies, and orchids. It will grow 4 to 5 feet tall on a thick, hollow stalk that supports long (2 to 3 foot), leathery leaves. As the plant matures, the tassel or pollen flowers will appear at the top, and from the leaf axils the small, sheathed ears will appear, with soft silk threads hanging from them. These are the female seed-bearing parts of the corn plant, the ones that receive the pollen. The ears will swell and develop into corn kernels along a central cob as pollination takes place. Suckers may also develop from corn plants, and sometimes they may even produce an ear. Usually two ears grow on each corn plant.

culture Corn must be kept weed free, and shallow cultivation is important until the tassels appear. Then stop cultivating. The extra "prop" roots will start to develop above ground as the corn matures, and these can be hilled up to give the plants extra strong footing. Side dress corn twice as it is growing, once when plants are about 6 inches high and again when they are about knee high. Spread a band of fertilizer along the row and work in lightly, using either 5-10-10 or 4-8-12 or a favorite organic high in phosphorus and potash. If corn leaves are yellowing or "firing," they need nitrogen. Watering will be important if the growing season is dry, especially after tassels form. Water deeply weekly if there is no rainfall.

harvest 2½ to 3 months. There is an old New England saying that "corn is picked when the cooking water starts to boil." Corn sugar will start to turn to starch as soon as the ear is taken from the plant. To capture the sweetest flavor, pick just before preparing dinner, or leave unhusked and refrigerate until cooking time.

pests *Corn ear worm:* A very destructive pest of corn that works its way down into the ears and destroys the kernels. Control with mineral oil squirted down into the silks, 3 to 7 days after they appear. Some of the newer varieties offer some resistance to ear worms: Honeycross, Seneca Chief, Spring Gold, Butter and Sugar.

European corn borer: Borers overwinter in corn stalks, so fall cleanup is essential. Delay planting of corn to miss the first brood, then plant the midseason varieties.

diseases *Corn smut:* A disfiguring parasitical fungus that forms large "boils" on stalks, leaves, tassels, or ears, prevalent in hot, dry weather. The case splits apart and spreads inky black dusty spores. At first appearance, the spore cases should be cut off and burned. It is essential to cut off the cases before they burst, as the spores are viable for 5 to 7 years.

111

cucumber

(Cucumis sativus)

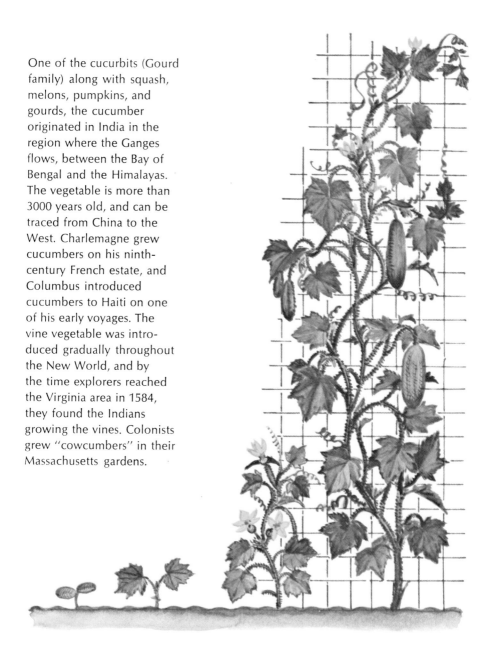

One of the cucurbits (Gourd family) along with squash, melons, pumpkins, and gourds, the cucumber originated in India in the region where the Ganges flows, between the Bay of Bengal and the Himalayas. The vegetable is more than 3000 years old, and can be traced from China to the West. Charlemagne grew cucumbers on his ninth-century French estate, and Columbus introduced cucumbers to Haiti on one of his early voyages. The vine vegetable was intro-duced gradually throughout the New World, and by the time explorers reached the Virginia area in 1584, they found the Indians growing the vines. Colonists grew "cowcumbers" in their Massachusetts gardens.

where to grow   Where a long, warm growing season, minimum 65 days, can be assured. Don't grow cucumbers where there are foggy, damp summers, as the plants are subject to mildews.

varieties   Since cucumbers are susceptible to many virus diseases and wilts, the selection of modern disease-resistant varieties is highly recommended. The following show resistance to all or many cucumber maladies: Marketmore Hybrid, Tablegreen 65; Spartan Valor; Marketer; Burpee Hybrid. All female (gynoecious) varieties: Gemini; Victory; Pioneer; Mariner.

Pickling varieties: SMR 18; West India Gherkin; Pioneer; Mariner

Burpless varieties: Burpless 26; Sweet Slice.

Tub-type varieties: Patio Pik; Cherokee.

Novelties: Lemon (fruit size and color of a lemon); China or Kyoto (an extra long cucumber).

soil   A fertile clay soil will support good cucumber growth if it is enriched with well-rotted manure and compost to aid its water-retentive qualities.

planting   Germination in 7–10 days.

When: Warm soil (65 degrees) is necessary for cucumbers to take hold. The plants are very susceptible to frost. Where there is a very short growing season, cucumbers can be planted in peat pots indoors a month to 6 weeks before planting outdoors. Cucumbers do not take readily to transplanting, and should be handled so that their roots are not disturbed. If there is ample garden space, the vines can be allowed to sprawl over the ground. Use a mulch of black plastic or straw or salt hay to keep the fruit clean. For small gardens, plan on training them to a trellis or support of some kind. This not only keeps the fruit clean and off the ground for quick ripening, but enables the fruit to grow straighter.

How: Where there is ample space and vines can sprawl, the simplest way is to plant cucumbers in hills, with several plants placed together. Space hills 4 feet apart each way and plant about 8 seeds per hill. Thin to the 3 strongest plants when the seedlings are about 4 inches high. Since cucumbers grow along rapidly once started, the ground should be prepared well in advance. Work a deep planting hole where each hill will be. Add a spadeful of well-rotted manure, and a generous handful of 5-10-10 or bonemeal and rock potash. Work in well and cover with soil before planting the seeds about an inch deep. The same soil preparation works well if the vines are to be trained on a support or grown in patio tubs.

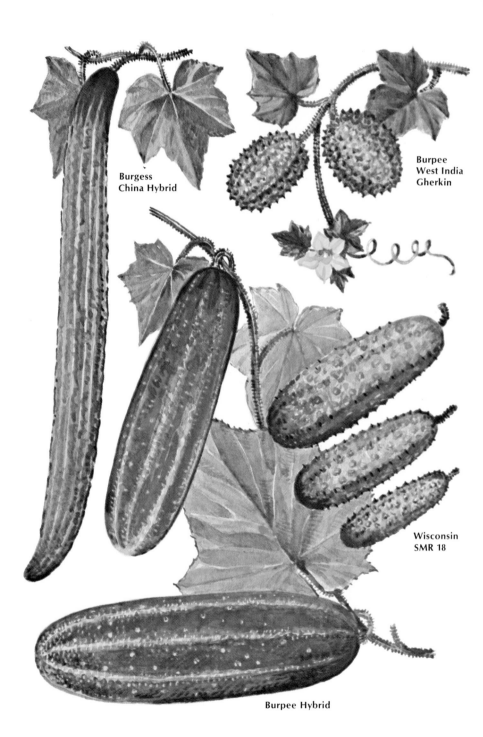

Burgess
China Hybrid

Burpee
West India
Gherkin

Wisconsin
SMR 18

Burpee Hybrid

how it grows   Once started, the cucumber vine grows along quite rapidly, putting out hairy stems with large, attractive leaves. The vines produce tendrils and can be trained to climb readily. The male (pollen-bearing) flowers will appear on the plant first, but do not produce fruit. A week or so later the female flowers appear, and produce the oval, elongated cucumber. The modern gynoecious (all-female) varieties are popular because they start bearing as soon as the first flowers appear. Seed packets contain enough of the good male pollen carrier to assure proper fertilization of these newer varieties.

culture   Once cucumbers start growing they must have a constant supply of soil moisture. If it is lacking, the plants stop growth in a "holding position" until there is more soil moisture. It is therefore important to grow cucumbers near a water supply. Keep weeds down with shallow cultivation or by growing the vines on black plastic mulch. Or mulch rows heavily with straw, salt hay, grass clippings, or partially rotted compost. When the plants are about 4 inches high, add a high-nitrogen fertilizer such as blood meal or cottonseed meal, or water the plants with fish emulsion. Avoid stepping on vines as they develop.

harvest   50 to 70 days. Never work around wet cucumber vines, as they are susceptible to many diseases that spread when leaves are wet. Since more than 50 percent of the cucumber is water, the fruit must be picked when it is succulent and green (immature) for best taste. If the fruit starts to turn yellow, it is past its prime and the seeds will be dark and ripe. It may be necessary to pick cucumbers daily as the harvest starts. If any mature cucumbers are left on the plants production will stop, so harvest carefully and remove any badly shaped or mature fruits.

pests   *Striped cucumber beetle (East Coast). Spotted cucumber beetle (West Coast):* This is essentially the same pest, which changes its coat depending on which coast it chooses. Adults overwinter on garden debris, so good fall cleanup is the first step in control. Or use diazinon or rotenone dust or try sieved wood ash.

Squash bug: Handpick adults and leaves bearing eggs. If boards are placed between rows in the evening, these insects will hide under them and can be destroyed in the early morning by uncovering and killing them.

Vine borers: These pests are usually not seen until the damage is done. Good fall cleanup to destroy overwintering eggs is important.

diseases   Grow resistant varieties.

eggplant
(Solanum melongena)

A member of the nightshade family,
along with peppers, tomatoes, and
potatoes, this beautiful vegetable has
been a staple in the Middle East and
India for centuries. The name is
derived from the egg shape of the
shiny, purple-coated fruit. There also
is an ornamental white eggplant, though
it is not commonly grown. In the
South, the plant is sometimes called
"guinea squash."

where to grow The plants require a long, warm growing season, as they are sensitive to cool temperatures and are killed by frost. Four months of 60–85 degree temperatures is the ideal climate. In the cooler spring climates, the plants must be started indoors. They can be grown successfully in containers in city gardens.

varieties Black Beauty; Black Magic Hybrid; Royal Knight; Burpee Hybrid; Jersey King Hybrid; New Hampshire. White Beauty is a novel, white-fruited variety.

soil A warm, loam soil enriched with compost or well-rotted manure.

planting Germination in 1 week to 12 days.

When: Start seed indoors to allow at least 10 weeks for young plants to develop. When the seedlings are about 3 inches tall, transplant them to individual peat pots; when they are about 6 inches high, they are ready to be planted outdoors. Harden off seedlings and plant outdoors when days and nights are warm.

How: In rows 3 feet apart, with 2 feet between plants. Where cutworms are a problem, protect seedlings with a paper collar. Each plant should bear an average of 4 fruits.

how it grows A rather decorative vegetable plant, with beautiful foliage and very lovely flowers growing from a strong central stem.

culture Water weekly if there is not sufficient rainfall; leaves will yellow if plants are not kept consistently moist. Feed every 4 weeks. Spread a small handful of well-balanced fertilizer in a circle around the base of each plant and scratch in very lightly. Do not overfeed, as this delays fruit set. The flowers are very beautiful, but no more than 4 to 6 fruits should be allowed to develop per plant. If too many flowers appear, pinch the extras off. Use mulches to keep weeds down.

harvest 80 days. A glossy coating on the fruit is a sign of readiness. Dull coatings or seeds that have turned brown indicate overripe fruits. Eggplants should be picked as soon as they are ripe. Because the stem is woody, cut, do not pull, the fruit from the plant. Store picked fruit in a cool place until it is eaten, but eggplant deteriorates rapidly, so don't wait too long to use.

pests *Colorado potato beetle:* Defoliates plants. Use Malathion.

diseases Eggplant is susceptible to the same verticillium wilt, a soil-borne disease, that affects tomatoes and potatoes. The best control is preventive: crop rotation. Do not plant eggplant where tomatoes, potatoes, or eggplant have been grown in the last 3 years.

fennel

(Foeniculum vulgare)

Fennel has been cultivated since ancient times both as a garden herb and vegetable and as a medicinal plant. It is native to Europe and Asia, where it became known for its aniselike flavor. Charlemagne grew sweet fennel, and the Anglo-Saxons used it for medicines. It has wide use today in commerce for candies, liqueurs, perfumes, and as flavoring.

There are three kinds: Sweet fennel *(F. vulgare)*, grown for its seeds and tender leaves; Florence fennel or finocchio *(F. vulgare dulce)*, grown for its bulblike base with a texture of celery; and, carosella *(F. piperitum)*, widely grown in Italy for flavoring.

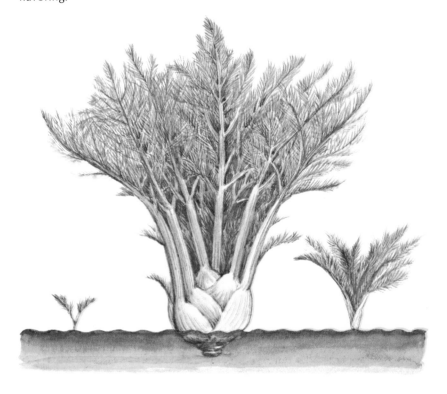

where to grow	Wherever a three-month frost-free growing season exists.
varieties	Mammoth is a fine variety of finocchio. Sweet fennel has no named varieties.
soil	Average garden soil that is well drained.
planting	Germination in 7–10 days.

When: When the soil is warm in the late spring. A second crop of finocchio fennel can be grown by starting another row a month after the first planting.

How: In rows 2 feet apart, seedlings thinned to 8 inches between plants.

how it grows	Sweet fennel sends up a tall, handsome plant resembling dill. It can reach a height of 5 feet in some instances. Finocchio, which is not as tall, has thickened leaves at its base that overlap to form a bulblike structure. This is the part that is cooked or used in salads.
culture	Keep the plants watered during dry periods. Finocchio should be hilled up slightly around the base of the plants when half grown to blanch the bulbs.
harvest	90 days.

For stems. Pick before the blossoms open.

For leaves: Pick when the yellow flowers open.

For seeds: Pick when leaves have turned brown.

For bulbs: Pick when well formed and properly blanched.

pests	None.
diseases	None.

horseradish

(Armoracia rusticana)

A curious condiment grown
for many centuries in
eastern Europe to provide
piquant flavor to meat
dishes. It was particularly
popular in Germany, and
later its use spread to
England. Colonists brought
it to this country, where
cultivated plants escaped
to the wild. It is used grated
and added to vinegar and
sauces for flavoring.
Although horseradish root
is sold commercially, home
gardeners may like to grow
their own, for the extra
freshness and for the
novelty.

where to grow Horseradish roots thrive best in a long, cool growing season, and do not succeed where summers are hot and dry.

varieties Maliner Kren and Bohemian.

soil Good friability is important so that the roots grow straight. Add lime if soil is very acid.

planting *When:* In spring, when the ground can be worked. The plant can become an aggressive weed, and for this reason many prefer to grow it as an annual and replant fresh roots every spring.

How: Young horseradish side roots are used for planting. They may be purchased commercially or saved from last year's plants. (If home roots are saved, cut the top end square and the bottom end slanted so the roots are set in the ground right side up.) The roots should be planted in rows 1–1½ feet apart, with 8 to 10 inches between roots. Set them vertically in the soil, 3 to 4 inches below the surface.

how it grows The entire plant grows about 2 feet tall and produces 18-inch-long leaves with wavy edges. Underneath the ground it forms a long parsniplike root with knobs or knots, plus several tiny side roots.

culture Keep weeds away from the plants and water weekly in dry weather. To grow a good root without side roots, "lift" the root twice. When the young leaves are 10 inches long, pull soil away from the top portion of the root and rub off small roots from the top and sides, leaving the strongest. Allow only the best sprout or crown of leaves to grow and remove all others. Replace soil. Repeat in 6 weeks or so to rub off any additional side roots that may have developed. Wear gloves to protect hands.

harvest The roots can be left in the ground until quite late in the fall, or they can be left until spring. Most gardeners prefer to dig them before the snow falls. They can be stored in a cool, dry place.

pests None.

diseases None.

jerusalem artichoke

(Helianthus tuberosus)

The Jerusalem artichoke is not an artichoke, but a sunflower; it does not come from Jerusalem and its edible portion is more like a potato than the true artichoke. Jerusalem artichoke was known and grown by the American Indians long before the settlers arrived in the New World. The plant is indigenous to North America, and is frequently found growing wild. It is usually listed in wild flower field guides. The term "Jerusalem" crept into the language as a corruption of the French *girasol* or Italian *girasole* for "sunflower." Further confusion is attributed to Samuel de Champlain, who when visiting Cape Cod noted that some roots given to him by the Indians tasted like artichokes. The Indians called them "sun-root." The tubers are starchless, carrying their type of carbohydrate in the form of inulin and levulan, which convert to levulose, a natural sugar.

where to grow   Anywhere the soil will suit them.

varieties   None have been developed.

soil   In the wild, they are usually found in damp, sunny fields.

planting   Tubers can be dug from the wild for planting or ordered from mail-order sources. A few nurseries sell them. They should be set in an out-of-the-way place in the garden where they will have room to grow and spread. If all tubers are not harvested carefully every fall, the plant can become an aggressive nuisance weed. If planted in rows, they should be at least 4 to 5 feet apart. Cut the tubers into sections with eyes, in the same manner as potatoes, and plant the pieces 2 feet apart.

how it grows   The plant is a tall, shaggy sunflower and grows to about 5 or 6 feet high, and even taller in favorable soil sites. The leaves are opposite, and the yellow flowers are about 3 inches wide. Tubers form in early fall and look like potatoes with knots.

culture   The plant is usually untended except for mulching. The plants need watering during dry spells. Some growers do apply high-phosphorus fertilizer after planting, but it is not essential.

harvest   3½ months. Wait until the plant flowers. When the flowers fade and drop, mark the calender and wait for another six weeks. Then the tubers should be dug and stored in a cool dry place. Be sure to find every tuber, or any remaining will take root and grow next year—and they may become a nuisance.

pests   None.

diseases   None.

kale
(Brassica oleracea acephala)

Kale, also known as borecole, is believed
to be a descendant of the wild form of
cabbage known to the ancient world. Like
its relative, collards, the leaves are nutritious,
and especially rich in vitamin A.

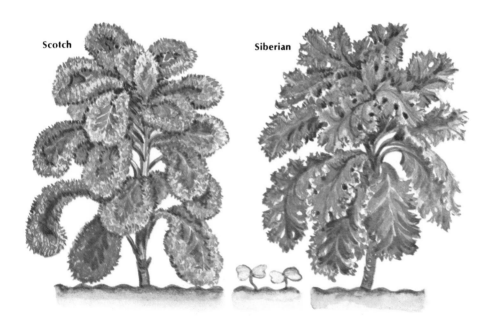

Scotch   Siberian

where to grow Almost anywhere in the United States where there is a cool fall growing season.

varieties There are 2 types: Scotch, an early kale with deeply curled, blue green leaves, (Dwarf Blue Curled), and Siberian, a later type with smoother, gray green leaves (Dwarf Siberian).

There also are ornamental kales, grown particularly for garden display in late summer and early fall when the annuals begin to wane. The leaves are deeply curled and beautifully tinted with pastel colors ranging from emerald green to soft lilac to reds and whites. The leaves may be eaten but are not as succulent as the crop varieties.

soil The ideal is a fertile, well-drained loam. Clay types can be improved with generous amounts of compost and well-rotted manure worked in to spade depth.

planting Germination in 7–10 days.

When: Start in midsummer for a late-fall winter crop.

How: In rows 18 inches to 2 feet apart. When the seedlings are 3 or more inches high, thin plants to 10 inches apart and use the thinnings for salads or as a cooked vegetable.

how it grows Like collards, kale develops attractive leaves from a central stem, which grows a foot or so tall.

culture Cultivate shallowly or mulch heavily to keep down weeds.

harvest 1 month. Leaf color is the best sign of crop readiness. Rich green leaves of firm texture are ready for cutting. If too dark and heavy, the leaves are tough and not as flavorful. Cut the leaves frequently. When cold weather begins, mulch the plants with straw, salt hay, or the like, they will continue producing well into winter, and they may even taste more flavorful.

pests Same as for cabbage.

diseases Same as for cabbage.

kohlrabi

(Brassica caulorapa)

Kohlrabi is probably the vegetable most suited in appearance for the space age. Its curious habit of growth—a tuber above ground radiating leafy stems—suggests a space satellite resting on earth before going into orbit.

Not much is known about kohlrabi's history until the early 1500s, when records show it was grown in Italian gardens. It spread through Europe gradually, then found its way into American gardens. Closely related to the turnip, some early records call it by its other name, stem turnip. A few botanists believe the plant is more closely related to cabbage marrow.

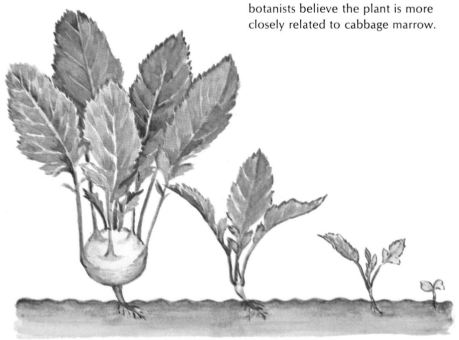

where to grow	Wherever turnips and cabbage will thrive.
varieties	Early White Vienna; Early Purple Vienna.
soil	A rich, fertile loam helps to produce the crop quickly, a must for good tender flavor.
planting	Germination in 5–7 days.
	When: After frost has passed. Succession sowing can be done every 2 weeks for continual harvest up to the end of July.
	How: Place seeds ½ inch deep in rows 18 inches apart, thin to 6 inches between plants.
how it grows	A very odd-looking vegetable, the plant produces its crop on top of the soil. A small, round turnip begins to form, with leaves resembling broccoli growing, spoke-fashion, in a circle around the bulb.
culture	The tuber tastes best if it develops quickly in constantly moist soil. This can be achieved with good mulching and watering whenever rainfall is scant.
harvest	55–60 days. The tubers have the best flavor if pulled up when they are about 2 to 2½ inches in diameter. Otherwise, they become hard and have a bitter taste.
pests	Same as for turnip.
diseases	Same as for turnip.

lettuce
(Lactuca sativa)

Of all the vegetables known to man, lettuce
is probably the oldest and most popular.
The Persian kings, who called it *kahn,* served
it on their royal tables as early as 550 B.C.
Aristotle praised it. The Chinese savored it.
Columbus took seed with him to Isabela
Island in the Bahamas.

The name "lettuce"can be traced to the
Old French *laitues,* meaning "milky," which
refers to the watery nature of the leaves.
The tall, broad-leaved cos or romaine
lettuce was developed in Italy; Rabelais
introduced it to France.

where to grow Practically anywhere. Since it is a cool-season vegetable, with an ideal temperature of 50–60 degrees, lettuce does poorly in hot weather. The leafy types mature quickly and are more suited for warm climates. Cos is also more heat tolerant.

varieties *Head:* Fulton; Ithaca; Big Boston.

Bibb: Buttercrunch; Summer Bibb.

Leaf: Black Seeded Simpson; Salad Bowl; Ruby; Oak Leaf; Slobolt; Grand Rapids.

Cos or Romaine: Parris Island.

soil An almost neutral soil is best with a pH of 6 or above. A rich, muck "celery" soil is excellent for lettuce, but the crop will do well in average garden soil. The best crops are grown in soil that is deeply enriched with well-rotted manure and is well-fertilized before planting, especially with high nitrogen—leaf-stimulating—fertilizers such as 10-8-4, cottonseed meal, or blood meal.

planting *When:* Early spring in regions where summers are hot, and again in late summer for fall crop. Head lettuce, especially, requires a long, cool growing season, and seed is usually started 6 weeks ahead. Transplants can be purchased. When sowing leaf lettuce, interesting rows can be made by mixing several varieties. As the crop wanes, a second sowing can be made or else it can wait until late summer, for fall.

How: Seed should be sown thinly in rows 1 foot apart; for leaf types, thin plants to 2–3 inches apart, then thin again by pulling every other plant when half grown. This will encourage thickly developed plants. For head, bibb, and cos types, space rows 18 inches apart, plants 8–10 inches apart.

how it grows Lettuce is about 95 percent water. It develops rapidly if the growing season is cool and moist. Head lettuce forms a tight, compact cabbage head from a dense rosette of leaves. Bibb develops a loose head of broad succulent leaves with superb flavor. Leaf lettuce has loose crispy or curly leaves that develop from a basal growing point. Cos and romaine also develop from a basal growing point, but the leaves are oblong and grow upright.

culture Since cultivation is difficult with these shallow-rooted plants, a mulch of grass clippings, salt hay, clean straw, or the like, will keep the weeds out and the growing soil moist and cool. Watering is essential if rainfall is scant. The plants need almost constantly moist ground.

Cos

Iceberg

Buttercrunch

Bibb

Ruby

Oakleaf

harvest   *Head:* 2 months. Pull the entire plant from the soil.

Bibb: 6–8 weeks. Pull the entire plant from the soil.

Leaf: 6 weeks and continually, since these are "cut and come again" plants. Cut the outer leaves when mature to allow center leaves to develop.

Cos: 2 months. Pull the entire plant.

pests   *Aphids:* Either grow nasturtiums near the lettuce, or if there is a heavy population, use rotenone or pyrethrum. Most minor infestations can simply be washed off before the plants are eaten.

Slugs: Place beer in shallow pans at dusk and empty the drowned slugs in the morning; or salt the nocturnal slugs as they feed and they will "dissolve."

diseases   Most of the blights and troubles have been eliminated through plant breeding and hybrid vigor.

melons

(Cucumis melo cantalupensis; Citrullis vulgaris)

Since their culture is almost the same, both cantaloupe and watermelon are grouped together.

The cantaloupe *(Cucumis melo cantalupensis)* is actually a vernacular name for a type of muskmelon. Other well-known muskmelons are honeydew, casaba, and Persian. The true cantaloupe is a warty Asian melon that was once brought by missionaries to Cantalupo, near Rome. Most botanists believe that muskmelons as we know them originated in Asia, particularly Persia and parts of India.

Watermelon *(Citrullus vulgaris)* was believed to be of Asian origin until David Livingstone explored central Africa and discovered watermelons growing wild there. Professionals then accepted its origin as African. The vines are grown extensively in Egypt and the Middle East.

where to grow Because melons require a long, warm growing season, their best production occurs in the South and Southwest, where there is ample growing time. Home gardeners in cooler regions can usually do fairly well with melons if they start seed indoors a month or more ahead of planting outdoors, but the vines need consistently warm days and nights to thrive. Melons take up enormous space, and should not be considered for the small vegetable plot.

varieties *Cantaloupes:* Mainerock Hybrid; Burpee Hybrid; Harper Hybrid; Saticoy Hybrid; Minnesota Midget (60 days).

Watermelons: The newer refrigerator-size small hybrids are more satisfactory for the average home garden, especially in the Northeast. Sugar Baby; New Hampshire Midget; Lollipop, red and yellow.

soil A sandy, light loam deeply enriched with manure and compost is ideal. Soil must be just slightly acid: pH 6. Since the vines are planted in hills, good yields are realized by working a spadeful of well-rotted manure and fertilizer such as bone meal into each hill before planting.

planting Germination in 7–10 days.

When: Because of the long growing season, start plants indoors 4 to 5 weeks before outdoor planting time. The soil must be warm and the weather settled with warm days and nights, as the plants are sensitive to cool. If nights are cool, use hot caps to protect the plants.

How: The vines do best if planted in hills. Rows and hills should be set 5 to 6 feet apart each way, with 2 or 3 plants per hill. Thin to the 2 strongest plants in a week.

how it grows Melons grow extensively broad, ground-hugging vines with soft, attractive foliage. The flowers appear quite suddenly, and it is interesting to watch the tiny melons start to develop after the flower petals drop.

culture The vines are heavy feeders, and also need adequate moisture as they start to develop. Give each hill about ½ cup of 5-10-5 fertilizer or liquid manure or fish emulsion 3 weeks after planting, and again (if you can find the original hill) after flowers appear. Keep the hills well watered up to the time fruit starts to fill out. Since weeding and cultivating are such problems with sprawling vine crops, black plastic or thick mulch proves an excellent aid to keeping weeds out, soil moisture in, and melons off the ground as they develop. The plastic mulch should be placed on the

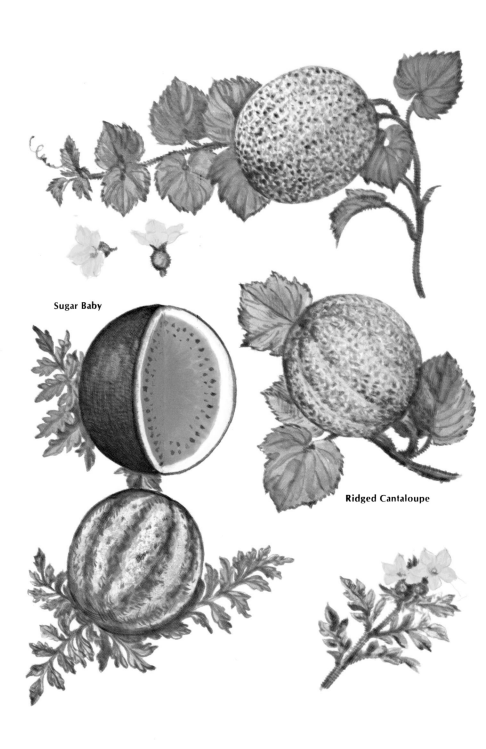

Sugar Baby

Ridged Cantaloupe

ground and anchored before planting, then central holes cut for the hills, with a few extra slits to let rain and hose water filter through.

harvest   3–3½ months for cantaloupes; 3 months for midget watermelons.

Cantaloupes: The easiest way to tell if they are ripe is a color test. The flesh between the netting turns to tan color from green. Also, if the melon slips off the vine easily with a gentle tug, it is probably ripe.

Watermelons: Determining ripeness takes talent. One method is thumping; a hollow dull sound when thumped with the thumb usually indicates ripeness. Or if the melon is turned over and the flesh is a deep yellow on the bottom, it is probably ripe.

pests   Same as for cucumber.

diseases   Same as for cucumber.

mustard

(Brassica juncea)

Popular in the South, this piquant, leafy vegetable deserves more garden growing. Originally from India, its culture spread to Burma and China, where it is still widely grown. The "grain of mustard seed" mentioned in the Bible was probably black mustard *(B. nigra)* or white mustard *(B. alba)*, which were grown primarily for the tiny seeds crushed to make table mustard. As a garden crop, mustard can be grown as leaf lettuce, using the younger, succulent basal leaves for salads, and cooking the more mature leaves the same as chard or spinach.

where to grow Chiefly in the South, but mustard can be grown almost anywhere.

varieties Southern Giant Curled; Tendergreen; Florida Broad Leaf; Fordhook Fancy; Green Wave.

soil Average soil that will support crops such as lettuce and radishes.

planting Germination in 3–7 days.

When: Where the growing season is long, 3 crops can be grown, with sowings in spring, summer and early fall. Otherwise plan on a spring and early fall crop.

How: In rows 1 foot apart, thin seedlings to 3–4 inches between plants.

culture Keep the plants well watered during dry spells, and cut the leaves frequently to prevent seed formation.

harvest 6 weeks. Cut the small basal leaves, as with leaf lettuce, and use raw in salads, or allow the leaves to develop further and cook like chard.

pests None of major importance.

diseases None of major importance.

okra

(Hibiscus esculentus)

A close cousin of the beautiful
tropical flower, hibiscus, this
curious vegetable comes from
Africa, where it was called
"gumbo." It traveled to Brazil in
the 1600s and arrived in Louisiana
with the French in the 1700s. A
traditional vegetable in Creole
cuisine, the pods are sliced
and used in stews and soups.
Thomas Jefferson, an appreciative
gourmet, knew the vegetable
and mentioned it in his *Garden
Book*. The ripened seeds are
sometimes used for coffee, and oil
from the seeds is a substitute for
corn or olive oil.

where to grow Okra is usually grown in the South, as the plants require warm soil and climate.

varieties Clemson Spineless; Emerald; Spineless Green Velvet.

soil Well-drained fertile soil enriched with rotted compost.

planting Germination in 10 days.

When: Okra is cold tender, and cannot be planted until the soil is warm and the air temperature well above 60 degrees.

How: Seed directly 1 inch deep, in rows 2½–3 feet apart. Thin tall varieties to 18 inches apart, dwarf varieties, to 12 inches.

how it grows A pretty garden plant with showy, small yellow hibiscus-type flowers and handsome foliage. Sometimes the tall varieties are grown as a garden hedge or border. Tall varieties grow to 4 feet; the dwarfs, to 2½ feet.

culture Keep weeds down by shallow cultivation, and side dress with a high-phosphorus–potash fertilizer after the seedlings are thinned.

harvest 60 days. Cut the seeds pods with a sharp knife, when they are no longer than 2 to 3 inches. The older pods develop tough, cellulose fibers. Okra can be sliced for stews and soups, boiled as a vegetable, or dipped and fried.

pests None of major importance except cotton pests, which sometimes invade okra plantings.

diseases None of major importance.

onion family
(Allium sp.)

Cooks could not accomplish very much in the way of
flavoring without this splendid group of plants,
which includes onions, garlic, leeks, shallots, and
chives (discussed under Herbs). There also are some
magnificent ornamental allium species grown for garden
display. Onions are believed to be prehistoric, and
even their native land is unknown. The Greek
historian Herodotus, in the fifth century, B.C., claimed
that an inscription on one of the pyramids gave the
sums spent for onions, radishes, and garlic eaten by the
slaves who built them. During their 40 years wandering
in the wilderness, the Israelites longed for onions,
leeks, and garlic. Leeks were worn in the hats of the
Welsh warriors to distinguish them from the
enemy in the confusion of battle. Today, the Welsh
wear leeks on Saint David's Day in commemoration of
the victory of their king, Cadwallader, over the
Saxons in 640.

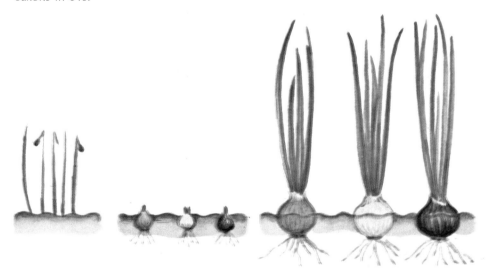

where to grow Onions prefer a cool-season start, and should have steadily moist soil and even growing weather to mature at a steady pace. Otherwise they bolt to seed or do not form good bulbs.

varieties see Planting below.

soil A fertile, mellow soil, well enriched with compost and rotted manures. The ground should be free of pebbles and stones and moisture retentive. Since onions are shallow rooted and need constant moisture to develop well, a well-balanced fertilizer should be worked in before planting.

planting *When:* Onions are relatively hardy, so planting can begin as soon as the soil is dried out and workable in spring. In milder climates, they can be planted in fall for spring harvest. If planted in too-cool weather, onions will not form bulbs.

How: Onions can be planted as seeds, sets, or plants.

Seed (for scallions, spring onions, or green onions): Varieties are Japanese Bunching; Southport White Bunching; Beltsville Bunching. There are also non-bulb-forming onions or Welsh onions *(Allium fistulosum).* Seed should be sown, in early spring to early summer, in rows 1 foot apart, then thin to 2–3 inches between plants. (Since these are shallow rooted, and ordinary thinning methods sometimes pull up too many plants, use a scissors to cut out too-thick plantings.)

Sets (year-old seedlings that were pulled when young bulbs and stored over the winter). Varieties are Ebenezer; Yellow Globe; Stuttgarter, or the local garden centers may just sell "white or yellow" sets. Place the sets in rows 1 foot apart, with 3–4 inches between the sets. Or put the sets closer and pull every other one for green onions or scallions, leaving the rest to mature for cooking onions.

Plants (seedlings raised in the Southwest, chiefly Texas, and shipped for planting when about 6–8 weeks or so old): These are sold by the bunch, and are the best way to start the large sweet onions, such as Sweet Spanish and Yellow Sweet Spanish. Bermuda types grown mainly in the South are Benny's Red, Crystal White Wax, and Yellow Bermuda. Plant in rows 1 foot to 16 inches apart, with 4–5 inches between plants.

how it grows The onion is a bulb-forming plant with long, tubular, deep, rich green leaves. They vary in size from the tiny green or spring onions to the large sweet Bermuda-type onion. Colors are white, yellow, and red.

Shallot

Garlic

Leek

Scallion

culture   Onions need fertile moist ground. Side-dress with fertilizer 2 to 3 weeks after planting and water well in any dry spells.

harvest   Seed 150 days; sets 100 days. Green or spring onions are pulled as needed when the stems are about ¼ inch thick.

For dry onions, those that will be dug and stored, the tops will start to yellow off and fall as the bulbs are maturing. If the entire row does not ripen uniformly, when the majority of onions are ripe knock down the foliage of the others with the back of a rake. Dig the onions carefully and allow them to dry in the open sun for a few days. Brush the soil off and cut the stem, leaving 2 to 3 inches attached, and store in a porous or net bag in a cool, dry place.

pests   *Thrips:* Malathion spray.

Onion maggot: Be alert for flies in spring; spray with malathion.

diseases   Buy quality sets and plants to be sure of clean stock.

garlic
(Allium sativum)   Garlic is simple enough to raise. Simply pull apart a garlic bulb, and plant the individual cloves about 2 inches deep and about 2 inches apart. Mature garlic bulbs should be ready in 3 months.

shallots
um ascalonicum
Allium cepa sp.)   Shallots, which are highly prized by French chefs, not generally available, and very expensive, are as simple to grow as garlic. The flavor reflects the quality of the soil, however, and since bitter taste seems to follow planting in clay soil, use typical good onion soil for shallots. The tops will start to brown off and yellow when the bulbs are mature, in about 90 to 110 days.

leek
(Allium porrum)   Unless noted otherwise below, leeks have the same needs as onions. Varieties are Broad London (Large American Flag); Swiss Special; Conqueror. Seed is usually sown indoors about 2 months before planting but can be seeded directly outdoors. Germination is in 10 days. Seedlings are set in a 6-inch trench, in rows 2 feet apart, with 6 inches between sets. The object of the trench is to blanch the leeks white as they grow; the row is gradually filled in as the leeks develop or the soil is merely hilled around the plants as they near maturity; but be careful not to brush soil into leaf stalks. Leeks should be pulled when fully mature, about an inch in diameter, in 120-130 days. In mild climates they can be left in the ground over winter and dug as needed. But in colder climates they should be harvested before frost, although some gardeners have been successful mulching leeks heavily and harvesting all winter.

parsnip
(Pastinaca sativa)

This nutritious root vegetable with its nutty flavor has been grown since ancient times. Parsnip is native to Europe and North America, and it is said that the Roman emperor Tiberius was so fond of the roots that he imported them from Germany. Foliage resembles that of carrot and the poisonous water hemlock. All three belong to the parsley family.

where to grow A long, cool, moist growing season is best, and for this reason the root does not succeed well in hot, dry climates.

varieties All-American; Harris Model; Hollow Crown.

soil Adequate deep soil preparation is the secret of success with parsnips, since the roots may go down as far as 18 inches. They thrive in deeply prepared loam soil enriched with generous quantities of compost and well-rotted manure. If the soil is too sandy, many extraneous fibrous roots develop; if too heavy, the roots fork. To prepare the soil, place the manure and compost on top and dig to the depth of a foot. A light application of 4-8-4 or 5-10-10 fertilizer or wood ash and ground phosphate rock can also be added at this time, and dug in so that the nutrients, deep in the soil, encourage the roots to grow down deeply to them.

planting Germination in 14–21 days.

When: The first part of May. Always use fresh seed.

How: Plant the seeds 4 to 5 seeds per foot, in rows 18 inches to 2 feet apart. Thin to 4–6 inches apart. Radish seed can be mixed with the seed to mark the row until the slow-germinating parsnips appear. Since parsnips are a long-maturing crop, lettuce or spinach can be planted between rows.

how it grows The foliage resembles the carrot, and eventually grows to 3 or 4 feet in height. The stems are hollow. The long white roots start to develop soon after germination, and then the tops grow full. Well-grown roots are about a foot to 15 inches long.

culture Unless the rows are heavily mulched to keep down weed growth and retain soil moisture, they must be cultivated lightly and frequently to keep weeds out. And whenever rainfall is scant, water generously once a week.

harvest 4 months. New Englanders believe parsnips are not fit to eat until spring—that when left in the ground over winter, the starchy roots become sweeter. They do improve after a few frosts. The roots should be dug, never pulled, and stored to be eaten during the winter months, or mulched heavily and left in the row through winter and dug in spring.

pests None.

diseases None.

peas

(Pisum sativum)

If gardeners could choose but a few vegetables to grow,
peas should be one of them. Like corn, nothing can
match the sweet, homegrown flavor of peas just
picked from the vine, shelled, and cooked. Approximately one-quarter of their weight is plant sugar,
sucrose, which deteriorates rapidly after picking or if
the pods overripen.

A native of Europe and Northern
Asia, the pea is an ancient
vegetable; seeds were found in
an Egyptian tomb at Thebes. It
was not generally grown until
the Norman conquest of England,
when records note its cultivation
in monastery gardens. Eventually
the English perfected the
vegetable, and colonists brought
fairly fine seed to the New World
with them. The Indians also
grew the legume. In the South
the pea is referred to as "English
pea" or "table pea," to distinguish
it from a favorite southern
vegetable, the black-eyed pea.
The recent popularity of Chinese
cooking has also spurred more
home gardeners to grow the
edible pod peas called
"snow peas" or
"sugar peas."

where to grow Peas are a cool-season vegetable, and do best in a climate where there are 2 months of cool growing weather, either spring planting in the northern regions or fall planting in the warmer southern regions.

varieties Peas have smooth or wrinkled seeds. Most of the varieties grown are wrinkled seed, since these are sweeter and more flavorful. The advantage of smooth seed is its toughness in withstanding rot in cold, wet soil, although many seedsmen now treat wrinkled seed varieties with a mild fungicide to prevent rotting.

Smooth seed: Alaska (55 days).

Early: Sparkle (60 days, dwarf); Frosty (64 days); Little Marvel (64 days, dwarf).

Midseason: Lincoln (67 days); Wando (69 days, heat resistant).

Late: Green Arrow (68 days, long pods); Alderman (74 days, long pods).

Edible pod: Little Sweetie (60 days, bush); Dwarf Gray Sugar (65 days, bush); Sweetpod (68 days, tall growing); Mammoth Melting Sugar (tall growing).

Field peas or cowpeas: California Blackeye (65 days); Brown Sugar Crowder (90 days).

soil Same as for beans.

planting Germination in 8 to 10 days.

When: The earlier the better. Seeds should be planted in the spring as soon as the ground can be worked. Do not plant in the hot summer months. Where winters are mild, a second fall crop can be planted in late summer, but where the summers are long and hot, this is not practical as the plants do not thrive, producing poor flowers and a disappointing crop. The simplest way to prolong harvest is to plant early, midseason, and late varieties at one time rather than sowing every 2 weeks.

How: Plant dwarf varieties about 8 seeds to a foot, about ½–1 inch deep; and in rows 18 inches to 2 feet apart.
Tall-growing varieties should be planted in double rows 4–6 inches apart, 2½ feet between double rows. Supports for climbing vines can be put in at planting time or just as seedlings are 3 inches high. For support use twiggy brush, chicken wire fencing, or weatherized trellis netting sold commercially for vine crops.

how it grows Peas grow on pretty vines to 3 and 4 feet tall; their pinnate leaves are topped by a curly trendril, which grasps onto a sup-

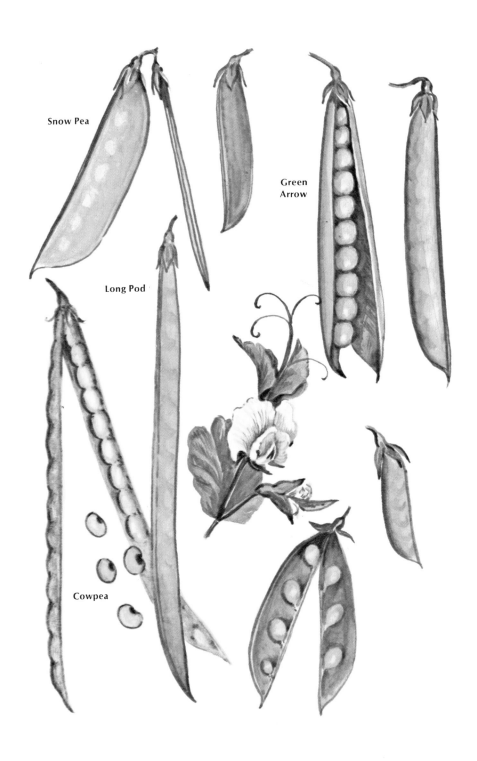

Snow Pea

Green
Arrow

Long Pod

Cowpea

port. The flowers are miniature sweet pea flowers, and pods begin to develop soon after the flowers drop. The dwarf peas do not grow taller than 2 feet, and do not need to be staked for support.

culture   Keep the rows weed free or mulch. After sowing, a thin line of fertilizer can be traced along either side of the row and worked in 3 to 4 inches from the plants. Too much nitrogen encourages foliage growth and not pods. Peas need constant soil moisture to keep developing well, and the ground should be watered when there is lack of rainfall.

harvest   60–70 days. When pods of the peas appear to be swelling with rounded pea forms, they are ready for picking. Take a test picking every day or so, and note the appearance of the pods with the sweetest peas. If the pods are left on the vines too long, they become tough and starchy. Pick the pods just before cooking, since they, like corn, deteriorate quickly after harvest. Choose a cool morning, not the heat of the day, or just after a cooling rain. The edible pod peas should be picked when the pods are well developed but before they become swollen with the outline of peas.

    Peas usually develop from the bottom of the vine up. Pull firmly but gently, and hold the vine with one hand so it is not jarred loose from its support when picking. When peas start to ripen pick them often, and pull all ripe pods present each time to encourage development of more pods; otherwise the crop stops developing. You can pick peas for about 2 weeks once they start coming.

pests   *Pea aphids:* rotenone or pyrethrum.

diseases   *Damping off:* Buy treated seed.

Downy mildew: Grow resistant varieties (Green Arrow).

Fusarium wilt: Grow resistant varieties.

pepper
(Capsicum frutescens)

The true pepper, companion of salt, comes
from a tropical vine, *Piper nigrum.* The
garden sweet or bell pepper and the hot,
spicy peppers are South and Central
American varieties grown extensively by the
Olmecs, Toltecs, and Aztecs long before the
New World was discovered. The spice-hungry
explorers were delighted to find the hot
peppers being grown in the West Indies and
Central and South America, and introduced
them to Europe and India in the sixteenth
and seventeenth centuries. From these
peppers come several culinary flavorings:
paprika, from a special type grown in
Hungary, tabasco from the tabasco pepper,
and the "pimiento" pepper used for stuffing
olives, among other things.

where to grow Peppers are strictly warm weather plants, and require at least 2½ months to mature, once started seedlings have been set outdoors. They will not produce where evenings are cool.

varieties Pepper is susceptible to mosaic, and where it is a problem, select mosaic-resistant varieties: Keystone; Belle; Staddon's Select; Yolo Wonder. Other good varieties are Ruby King; Sweet Banana; Calwonder. Hot peppers: Hungarian Wax; Hot Portugal; Long Red Cayenne.

soil A sandy, well-drained loam is best. Add a well-balanced fertilizer such as 5-10-5 or a favorite organic blend and work in well.

planting Germination in 2 to 3 weeks.

When: Start peppers indoors at least 2 months before they are transplanted outdoors, then set outdoors after the days and nights are warm, otherwise the plants yellow and stop growing.

How: In rows 2 feet apart; with 18 inches between plants. At planting time mix about 2 tablespoonfuls of a well-balanced fertilizer in the planting holes and water well after planting. (Grow hot peppers separately to prevent cross pollination with sweet bell peppers.)

how it grows Pepper is a decorative plant, about 2½ feet tall with handsome leaves, and at blooming time, a display of pretty white flowers. An ideal vegetable for patio growing, pepper can be mixed in flower borders or raised planters. If too many flowers form, the plant will naturally discard those not going to bear fruit.

culture Similar to eggplant; peppers need constant soil moisture once growing begins. Hill up soil around the base of the stems gradually to give the stems added support when bearing the fruit. Keep weeds away with shallow cultivation, or use mulches. Feed the plants again when flowers fade and fruits are forming.

harvest 70 to 80 days. Sweet peppers are picked green, not fully ripe. They will feel firm and crisp when ready, and should not be pulled from the plant but cut with a sharp knife. Peppers will keep in the refrigerator for about 2 weeks after picking before they start to shrivel. If left on the plant, peppers turn ripe red and the flesh is sweeter. If frost threatens, pull up the plant and hang it in a cool place to allow peppers to ripen.

Hot peppers should ripen fully on the vine to attain their bright red color and full flavor. Then hang to dry.

pests None of major importance.

diseases None of major importance.

potato

(Solanum tuberosum)

Though a relatively modern vegetable, the potato is practically a world food staple except in Asian countries. The plant comes originally from South America, where it was grown by the Peruvian Incas, who called it *patata*. Spanish explorers are credited with its introduction to Europe, although it was the Irish who were among the first to grow it extensively. Historical tales attribute Sir John Hawkins or Sir Walter Raleigh with having introduced the potato to Ireland. The food staple was brought to America when Irish emigrants settled in New Hampshire in 1719. The potato blight that caused the Irish famine in 1846–1847 also brought more Irish emigrants to America, along with their culinary customs. Only those who have the garden space, long, cool growing season, and fertile soil should venture the potato, a member of the nightshade family along with tomatoes and peppers.

where to grow	In regions where there is a temperate climate with cool growing weather, ample rainfall, and deep, fertile soil.
varieties	"Seed" potatoes that have been certified disease free are essential. Supermarket potatoes are usually treated to prevent sprouting, and will not grow if planted.
	Early: Irish Cobbler; Chippewa; Norland (scab resistant); Pontiac (red-skinned)
	Main: Green Mountain; Katahdin; Kennebec (blight resistant)
	Baking: Russet Burbank
soil	A deeply fertile sandy loam with a high acid content, ph 5–5.5, is best, since overly limed soils activate the scab fungus. Use high-phosphorus fertilizers, such as 5-10-5, 4-8-4, or ground-rock phosphate to prepare the soil.
planting	*When:* As soon as the frost is out of the ground and the soil can be worked thoroughly.
	How: Seed potatoes are often precut and pretreated. Each piece should have 1 to 2 "eyes," which will give rise to the plants. Plant "seed" 10–12 inches apart, 3–4 inches deep in rows 3 feet apart.
how it grows	The plants, which are about 3 feet high, send up long, pinnate leaves similar to tomato foliage. The tubers will develop in late summer, at the ends of underground stems. They are fairly close to the top 4 to 5 inches of soil.
culture	Keep weeds out of the potato patch with very light cultivation, or use straw or leaf compost mulch. Gradually hoe soil toward the base of the potato plants, to prevent the roots from becoming sunburned. A second application of fertilizer is usually made 1 month after planting by side dressing it in the row. Potatoes are almost three-quarters water; soil moisture is important.
harvest	2½–4 months. The first young potatoes can be lifted out carefully, a few at a time, by merely pulling soil away and replacing it for the remainder to develop. When the plants begin to dry and die down, the tubers will be ready. They can be left in the ground for a time, but should be dug before a heavy frost. Dig on a bright, sunny day so the soil dries off the potatoes easily.
pests	*Colorado potato beetle:* A small yellow beetle with black lines down its back that produces one or two generations of havoc with potato crops. Control by handpicking and/or diazinon dust.
	Leafhopper: Leaf-sucking insects. Diazinon dust.
diseases	*Blights and scabs:* Grow resistant varieties and do not overlime.

153

pumpkin
(Cucurbita maxima)

The pumpkin is just a big, overgrown squash. Indeed, most of the commercially canned "pie" pumpkin is squash. The name stems from the French, *popon,* derived from the Greek *pepon.* The French explorer Jacques Cartier described the *gros melon* growing along the shores of the St. Lawrence River, and Captain John Smith mentions the *pompions.* Squash can be distinguished from pumpkins by their stems. The squash will have rounded, rather tender stems, while the pumpkin stems are rougher, rather square, and almost woody. Where there are children in the family, there is an excuse for growing pumpkin, either for Halloween or to enter one of the state fair "big pumpkin" contests. If garden space is limited, this wide-spreading squash is best left to farmers who have the field room to spare.

where to grow   Wherever there is room to spread. A frost-tender plant, it requires at least 3½ months growing season to mature.

varieties   Small 7-inch types: Jack-O'-Lantern; Big Max; Connecticut Field; Small Sugar; Spookie. Lady Godiva, a new USDA development that is grown for its edible naked hull-less seed and not the pumpkin flesh.

soil   Fertile, well enriched with rotted compost and manures.

planting   Germination in a week to 10 days.

When: As soon as the soil is warm and the climate settled.

How: Plant 4 to 5 seeds in hills spaced at least 8 to 10 feet apart. When the seedlings germinate, thin to the best 2 per hill. Where garden space is limited, plant 1 or 2 hills.

how it grows   Similar to all squash but a more aggressive spreader. Flowers form late in the summer, and the small pumpkins start to form soon after.

culture   Same as for squash. For giant contest-winning pumpkins, eliminate all but a flower or two per vine, and allow just a pumpkin or two to develop.

harvest   3½ months. Cut, don't pull, the ripe pumpkin from the plant in time for Halloween or the state fair contest. But be sure to harvest the pumpkins from the field before frost.

pests   Same as squash.

diseases   Same as squash.

radish

(Raphanus sativus)

Along with turnips and onions, the
radish is one of the oldest vegetables
known to man. The Egyptian pharaohs
esteemed it, and the Greeks made
offerings to Apollo of radishes
fashioned in beaten gold. The English
used it as a "sauce with meates to
procure appetite," and the Massachusetts Bay colonists grew it in their
new gardens. The plant is best known
in Asia, among the Japanese and
Chinese, who use it as a winter
vegetable. In America it is chiefly
a relish.

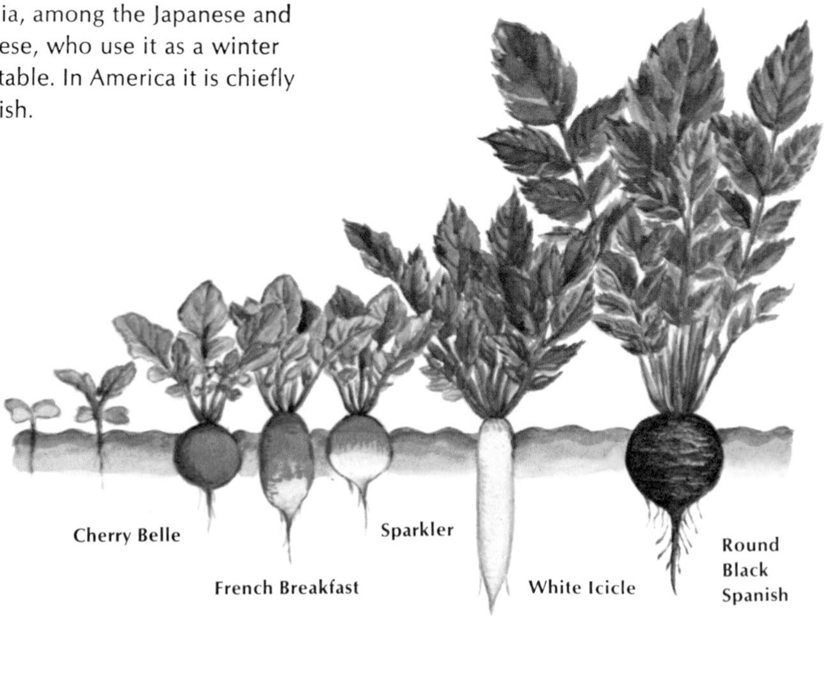

Cherry Belle

French Breakfast

Sparkler

White Icicle

Round
Black
Spanish

where to grow Radishes are a good beginner's vegetable, and especially appealing for children's gardens. While they do not grow well in hot weather, they do grow in practically any kind of soil, and are ready to harvest in 21 to 28 days. The seed thrives in gardens, planters, terrace boxes, and even in windowsill pots. It can also be planted as a winter greenhouse crop.

varieties There are basically 3 kinds: spring, summer, and winter.

Spring (globular): Cherry ·Belle; Champion; French Breakfast; Sparkler.

Summer (long rooted): White Icicle; Crimson Giant (red).

Winter (long maturing radishes stored for winter use): White Chinese; China Rose; Round Black Spanish.

soil Grows well in average garden soil.

planting Germination in 3–7 days.

When: Sow spring varieties as soon as the ground can be worked, then again every week up to midspring for succession crop. Sow again in August for a late summer–fall crop. Sow winter varieties in midsummer for a late fall crop, which is stored for winter use.

How: Set seed ½ inch deep in rows 1 foot apart, then thin to 1 inch apart for spring radishes and 3 inches for winter radishes.

how it grows The root swells quickly into a crisp, succulent vegetable. Because of their quick germination, radishes are often sown as a companion crop to such slower-growing crops as carrot to mark the row and simplify thinning.

culture Keep the rows weed free. Radishes are tasty and crisp if grown rapidly with ideal soil moisture and fertility. If the ground is too wet and soggy, they often crack. If the soil is too dry during the growing season, the roots become pithy.

harvest Summer varieties are usually ready in 3 to 4 weeks. The tops of the red globular radishes often push above the ground when the crop is ripe. If the roots are left in the ground too long, they become woody. Winter radishes require the long, cool growing season to develop into crisp roots. When ready, they are pulled and stored in moist sand at temperatures just above freezing.

pests *Cabbage maggot:* Tunnels into roots, making them inedible. Use a soil drench of diazinon just before seeding new rows.

diseases None of major concern.

rhubarb
(Rheum rhaponticum)

Originally a medicinal plant,
rhubarb dates back to 2700 B.C.
in China. The present sort is
believed to have originated in
the desert region of Siberia
around the Volga River. It was
introduced to Europe in the
seventeenth century, and
gradually found its way to
America, where New Englanders
frequently called it "pie plant."
Grown for its red, acid-flavored
stalks, this is a rewarding
perennial that demands little
care. A few plants will supply
ample stalks for pies, rhubarb
sauce, and fruit stews.

where to grow	In the cool northern states where there is a cool spring to mature its stalks and a cold winter, required for its dormant period.
varieties	MacDonald; Victoria; Valentine; Canada Red.
soil	A deeply prepared fertile soil that drains well. Since this is a long-lived perennial, good soil preparation before planting will assure long years of harvest. Generous quantities of humus, well-rotted compost, and bone meal, or a well-balanced fertilizer such as 5-10-5, should be added.
planting	*When:* In the spring, as soon as the ground can be worked.
	How: Rhubarb root divisions—a strong piece of root and a few buds or stalk shoots—should be set 3 to 4 inches deep, with a 4-foot spread each way. Since rhubarb is a perennial, you should choose a corner or place in the garden where its decorative foliage can be an asset.
how it grows	Rhubarb starts to send up its red tip shoots in early spring, then enormous green leaves, which can be 2½ feet wide, develop. The leaf stalks, or edible portion, are bright red. The plant is rather handsome, and need not be hidden out of sight.
culture	Rhubarb is not very demanding if the soil is well prepared before planting. A side dressing of fertilizer can be added in early spring when the stalks are beginning to appear, or feeding can be done after the crop is harvested to spur a good crop for the next year. In climates where winters are severe, a mulch of rotted manure and straw is helpful, but remove it in early spring.
harvest	Plants will last 10 to possibly 15 years. No stalks should be harvested the first year, and then only a few the second year. By the third season the plants will be well established. The stalks are pulled up from the plant with a quick jerk, never cut.
warning	Never eat the leaves of rhubarb, cooked or raw. They contain oxalic acid and are poisonous.
pests	None.
diseases	None.

rutabaga
(Brassica napobrassica)

Often called "Swede turnip," in many ways
the rutabaga is just an oversized turnip.
But there are specific differences. The
rutabaga requires a month longer to grow
and its foliage is more like that of the
cabbage, with glaucous, smooth leaves
instead of the rough leaves of the turnip.
Also, the root itself is rounder and firmer
than the turnip, and many say its flavor is
more interesting. But essentially the
culture for both plants is quite the same.

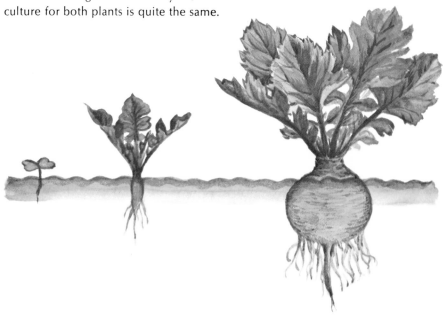

where to grow   Essentially a cool-weather vegetable.

varieties   American Yellow Top (yellow flesh); Macomber (white flesh).

soil   Average garden soil, enriched with compost and a high-phosphorus fertilizer, such as 5-10-5 or 5-10-10 or ground phosphate rock, to encourage good root development.

planting   Germination in 6–7 days.

When: Wait until June or early July to sow the seed, as the roots do not develop well in the heat of summer.

How: In rows 2 feet apart, thin plants to 1 foot apart.

how it grows   Similar in looks and shape to the turnip, although it develops more slowly; on the whole, the root is a bit rougher looking than the smooth turnip. The foliage is green blue.

culture   Same as for turnip.

harvest   90 days or 3 months to maturity. The roots are mature when about 3 inches thick. Unlike turnips, which deteriorate if left in the ground too long, rutabagas can be stored in the ground if well mulched and dug as needed. The flavor is better after a few frosts.

pests   Same as for turnip.

diseases   None of major concern.

salads

Even with the tiniest plot of ground, some space should be saved for the salads. These are the unusual and different leafy crops that provide interesting flavoring, color, and amusement for cooks and gourmets. They are all reasonably simple to grow, provided there is fertile, well-drained soil that is not going to pack hard. Constant moisture, but not soggy ground, will support a bountiful crop, and full sun and freedom from weed competition are also important. If the salad greens are to be planted in rows, space them about a foot apart. And remember to thin the rows after seedlings are about 3 inches high to allow growing space for the plants.

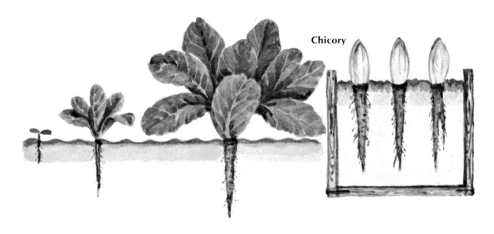

Chicory

chicory This is the elegant Witloof or blanched celery-heartlike vegetable
(Cichorium commonly, though erroneously, called French or Belgian endive.
intybus) Growing is a two step process: the roots are grown and harvested
like parsnips, then planted in a warm, dark place and "forced" to
develop the edible tops.

Plant the seed in early summer and allow the roots to develop
for the entire summer, keeping the rows weed free. The tops, which
are not eaten, will resemble cos lettuce. In late fall pull up the
roots. Trim off the tops, leaving a 2-inch stub, and cut the roots
to a uniform length, about 6–8 inches. Plant the roots in a deep
wooden box or bushel basket filled with about 4 inches of moist
soil. Space fairly close together. Fill in to bury the leafy stubs
with about 6 or 7 inches of sand, and moisten thoroughly. Keep
in a warm, dark place, usually the cellar, and in about 3 weeks,
the blanched chicory heads will start to push through. They are
ready to eat when about 4 to 5 inches tall.

Radichetta, or cicoria, a sharply flavored chicory with toothed
leaves can be also grown for salad greens.

Magdaburgh chicory is ground to flavor coffee, popular in the
South.

corn salad Often called "lambs' lettuce," "field salad," "mache," or
(Valerianella "doucette," this is a rarely grown cool-weather salad green with
olitoria) bland flavor and pale green spatulate leaves about 3 inches long.
It grows best if planted in the cool growing months for a quick
crop. Kept lightly mulched, it will grow well into the winter and
even spring months in milder climates. A related form is Italian
corn salad.

watercress A dark green aquatic plant with pungent flavor, watercress is
(Nasturtium often used as a garnish as well as for salads. The plants grow
amphibium) best if they are set out in a low, sandy-bottomed stream of fresh
water. Seed is sown in a pot of soil and set in a pan of water
for constant moisture, then the seedlings are transplanted to a
stream when 3 inches high. Attempts are often made to grow
watercress by setting the pots in tubs of water, but this is not
always successful.

garden cress Pepper-grass is another name for this delightful parsleylike plant
(Lepidium with its sharp flavor, suggesting watercress, that adds to every
sativum) salad. Anyone can grow it—in a garden, in a pot, on a sunny
window sill. It germinates quickly and can be kept growing year
round. Thin plants to about 3 inches apart, and when they are
6 inches tall, snip off the tops and a second growth will follow.

Upland Cress

Corn Salad

Garden Cress

Roquette

Dandelion

Endive

Sorrel

Watercress

upland cress
(Barbarea verna)

Suggesting watercress in flavor, upland cress can be grown without a stream of running water. Grow it in the cool fall months and keep the soil moist.

dandelion
(Taraxacum officinale)

Be alert in spring, when the lawn becomes dotted with the first growth of this ubiquitous weed. The young, succulent leaves have the best flavor. After they mature, they become tough and bitter.

endive
(Cichorium endivia)

There are two types of this popular salad green, the deeply curly and slightly bitter type sometimes called "chicory," and the broad-, flat-leaved, more bland-tasting type called "escarole." Both are grown the same way as lettuce. Sometimes the commercial varieties are blanched white at the heart, but in the home garden this is not necessary.

roquette
(Eruca sativa)

Several names identify this famous European salad green: rocket, rugula, arugula, or erucola. It has a distinct, sharp flavor that should be mixed with other salad greens. Sow in spring or fall, as it is not a hot-weather grower.

sorrel
(Rumex acetosa)

A cousin of the weed dock, this early spring green with a mildly sour flavor is most popular with the French for soup. A perennial, once planted it can be nurtured for many seasons, but should be mulched and not allowed to go to seed as it can become a weed nuisance. The leaves are considered by some to be a good substitute for spinach.

salsify

(Tragopogon porrifolius)

A curious plant quite similar to
the parsnip in appearance, it is
grown for its flavorful roots,
which suggest oysters when baked,
fried, or boiled. Some call it
"oyster plant" or "vegetable
oyster." A plant of the Mediterranean regions and Asia Minor,
it did not reach America until
the nineteenth century. A similar
plant, black salsify (Scorzonera
hispanicus) is slightly larger
and noted for its black skin
and white flesh. Both plants
belong to the sunflower family.

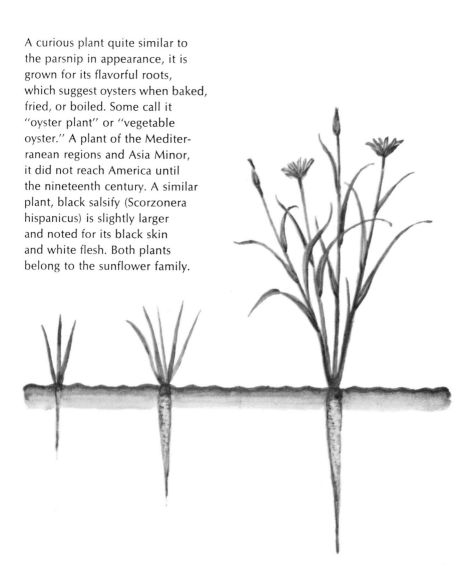

where to grow   Where there is a long season of steady growing weather. New Englanders do not seem to be too successful with it.

variety   Mammoth Sandwich Island (white).

soil   Similar to the soil required for parsnips, deeply and well prepared with compost for long root growth, and with the addition of a high-phosphorus–potash fertilizer such as 5-10-10. A slightly acid reaction pH 6 is best.

planting   *When:* In spring, when the ground can be worked.

How: Sow seed directly in rows 1 foot apart; then seedlings thinned to 3–4 inches apart. Since the crop takes four months to mature, radishes or lettuce can be interplanted in the row where space is at a premium.

how it grows   The roots when mature are about 8 inches long and about 1½ wide at the top, tapering narrowly like a carrot. The roots are skinnier than parsnips, and the tops have long, linear leaves with a purple flower. Black salsify is slightly larger.

culture   Similar to parsnip.

harvest   4 months. Roots can be left into the ground until late fall, or mulched and used during the winter months. Dig, do not pull them up.

pests   None.

diseases   None.

soybean

(Glycine max)

This ancient plant, dating back to
5000 B.C., has long been a staple in
Chinese culture. It is nutritious, high
in protein and low in carbohydrates,
making it an important food source.
It became known in the West after
missionaries returned to Europe from
China in the eighteenth century.
Ben Franklin sent seeds home while
he was in France, and Admiral Perry
brought seeds back with him
from Japan.

The soybean is now a crop of high
commercial importance. Its seeds are
used for oils, the manufacture of
plastics, margarine, soaps, and paints.
This legume has been known to
farmers for some time as a green
manure crop to renew worn soils. There
is current interest in soybeans as a
natural food of high nutritional value.

where to grow	Like all true beans, a warm growing season in fertile soil is needed.
varieties	Edible Verde; Kanrich, a dwarf type.
soil	A fertile, well-drained soil that would support a bean or pea crop.
planting	*When:* When the soil is warm and frost is out of the ground. Since the soybean is a legume, an inoculant may be helpful if this crop has not been grown on the soil before. Inoculants are inexpensive and available at most garden supply stores. *How:* 1½ inches deep, in rows 2 feet apart; thin seedlings to 12–18 inches between plants.
how it grows	Soybean is a bushy plant that grows to a height of 3 or 4 feet; it has rough hairs on its stems, leaves, and pods. A prolific plant, its pods resemble pea pods and contain 2 to 4 seeds.
culture	Keep the rows weed free and stay out of wet soybeans until the sun dries the plants.
harvest	100 days. Young soybeans resemble baby limas, and can be eaten at this stage or left on the plant to mature as dried beans, or as sprouts (see Sprouting, page 000). Soybeans are difficult to shell; soak them in boiling water for 5 minutes and then pop the beans out of the end of the pod.
pests	None of major concern in a home garden.
diseases	None of major concern in a home garden.

spinach
(Spinacia oleracea)

This leafy, deep green vegetable rich with
vitamin A traveled from Iran with the
Moors to Spain and then to the gardens of
Europe and eventually the Americas.
Because it has such a distinct flavor, there
are many who prefer it cut up raw for
tossed salads rather than cooked. The deeply
crinkled leaves harbor sand and soil grains,
and must be washed thoroughly.
Soaking them in lightly salted water seems
to draw the particles to the bottom.

New Zealand Spinach

Bloomsdale

where to grow Where there is at least a month and a half of cool growing weather. The plant bolts to seed in warm weather.

varieties Winter Bloomsdale; America; Viking. For hot weather "spinach" there are several substitutes: New Zealand "spinach" (*Tetragonia expensa*), a plant discovered in New Zealand by Captain Cook, is grown as a summer crop. It has short, arrowhead-shaped leaves with good flavor. Malabar and Tampala are also succulent-leaved summer "spinach."

soil Spinach should have very fertile, well-drained soil that holds moisture readily. This will assure the fast growth needed for crisp, tender leaves. The pH should be close to neutral 6.5 to 7. Acid-type soils should be limed.

planting Germination in 7–10 days.

When: As soon in the spring as the ground can be worked. The ground can be prepared in the fall and covered with plastic mulch so that it is ready early in the season. In some instances, a fall-sown spinach crop, well mulched, will winter over and start growth again in spring.

How: In rows 12 inches apart, seedlings to 3 inches between plants. (New Zealand spinach is a large-growing plant and needs 2-foot rows, 1 foot between plants. Soak seed overnight before planting because it germinates slowly.)

how it grows Clusters of heavy, deep green leaves, deeply crumpled or savoyed, form from a central crown. If the season turns suddenly warm for a long period, the plants will bolt, put up a flower stalk, and go to seed.

culture Once planted the crop must grow along rapidly. Be sure the rows are kept moist if spring or fall is dry, and side dress with a high-nitrogen fertilizer such as blood meal or fish emulsion when seedlings are 3 inches tall.

harvest 45 days. Cut spinach plant off at the base when the leaves are fully developed. Once cut, they will not "come again," like chard and lettuce. New Zealand spinach sprawls vigorously; when the stems are about 8 inches long, the tip ends should be cut several inches to keep it under control. Cook or use as leaf lettuce mixed in salads.

pests Aphids may be troublesome. In mild climates, nasturtiums nearby will help draw the insects away. Or use pyrethrum or rotenone dust.

diseases *Blights:* Grow the modern resistant varieties.

171

squash
(Cucurbita sp.)

Squash are Western Hemisphere plants, grown long
before the explorers from the Old World reached
the new lands. Two types are grown: summer squash
(Cucurbita pepo) and winter squash *(C. maxima* and
C. moschata). Summer squash, which are eaten
when immature, were popular with the Indians.
Roger Williams, the founder of Rhode Island, described
this Indian vegetable as "vine apples of several
colors." The name "squash" is taken from the Indian
work *askutasquash,* meaning "eaten raw or uncooked."
The larger winter squash with hard rinds of warty
or rough texture came from the Andes mountains, and
were unknown to European culture until the sixteenth
century. Squash has never had wide popularity in
Europe except in the warmer growing climates like that
of Italy, where zucchini and cocozelle are popular.
In England, squash are called "vegetable marrow."

where to grow   Summer squash can be grown almost anywhere, as the vines develop quickly. Harvest begins in 2 months.

Winter squash require a longer growing season and more garden space for sprawling plants. They do not thrive in hot, dry regions where there is limited water supply.

varieties   *Summer:* Zucchini Elite; Seneca Prolific (yellow); White Bush Scallop and Patty Pan; Gold Neck Hybrid.

Winter: Waltham Butternut; Buttercup; Golden Delicious; Hubbard; Table King (acorn).

soil   A light, fertile soil deeply enriched with well-rotted manure and compost to retain soil moisture, or with a well-balanced fertilizer before planting; squash are heavy feeders.

planting   *When:* When the soil is warm and the air temperature settled. Squash are susceptible to frost and cool weather. If the growing season is very short, seed can be started indoors in peat pots for transplanting outdoors 6 weeks later.

How: The hill method is simplest, since the soil can be deeply prepared for each hill before planting. A good spadeful of well-rotted manure and/or compost should be dug in, then water the soil well.

Summer squash hills should be spaced 3 feet apart each way; plant 6 or 7 seeds per hill and thin to the 3 strongest seedlings when the plants are 3 inches high. Or the seeds can be planted sparingly in rows three feet apart and thinned to 2 feet apart.

Winter squash hills should be spaced 6–8 feet apart each way; thin to the 3 strongest plants when the seedlings are 3 inches high.

how it grows   Squash are spreading, vinelike plants with wiry, curly tendrils. Summer squash are more compact-growing types called "bush." The leaves are large, shaped somewhat like a maple leaf. The five-petaled squash flowers are very beautiful, with their yellow orange colors. Soon after the flowers wilt, the squash start to develop. Summer squash ripen in several days; winter squash take much longer to develop.

culture   The squash area should be kept weed free while the plants are young. Black-plastic or very heavy mulch is practical for such spreading vine plants, as weeding is difficult. Feed twice, immediately after thinning to the 3 strongest seedlings and again just before the vines start to "run." The plants must have adequate moisture all through the growing season. Note: The popular

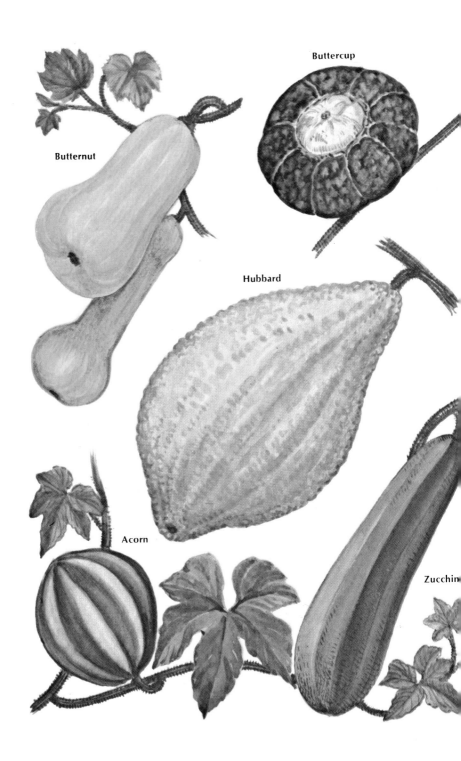

Buttercup

Butternut

Hubbard

Acorn

Zucchini

rotation that squash and melon cross-pollinate each other is a fallacy.

harvest   *Summer:* 60–70 days. These squash are picked immature before they are fully formed. The skin must be soft and tender, otherwise the squash will be overripe and of poor quality. Check squash plants almost daily when they start to flower, as the fruit will develop in 2 or 3 days in hot growing weather. The vines must be kept picked or the plants will stop producing.

Winter: 90–120 days. When the stems turn a light green yellow color, the squash should be fully ripe. The rind will be thick and tough. Cut, do not pull, the ripe fruit from the plant. Two to 3 inches of stem end must remain for proper storing. Some gardeners find it helps to ripen the squash in the sun for a few days before storing. This may increase the sugar content.

pests   *Squash bug:* Pick the red-brown egg clusters when seen or use pyrethrum or rotenone. The insects can be trapped under boards set out at night and the pests destroyed in the morning.

Squash vine borer: Undetected until a vine suddenly wilts, it tunnels into the stem. The entry hole can usually be noted by the presence of excrement. Cut into the stem with a razor to kill the borer, then hill the plant stem up thoroughly so it can reroot and continue growing.

diseases   None of major importance.

sweet potato

(Ipomoea batatas)

The sweet potato is a warm-weather crop
that requires a large amount of space to
spread out. Commercial growers seem
to have conquered its cultural necessities,
and therefore it is to the supermarket
produce (or even canned) supply most
gardeners will turn. But if you insist, here
it is. The sweet potato is not related to
the potato but is part of the morning glory
clan. Columbus discovered it in the West
Indies, and the Spanish conquistadores
introduced it to the Philippines and
the Pacific Islands. In this country sweet
potato is particularly popular in the South,
where the moist-fleshed tubers are
called "yams." The true yam is an unrelated
species, *Dioscorea.*

where to grow   Wherever a minimum of four months of warm growing season can be satisfied. Do not attempt to grow in northern states.

varieties   Centennial; Porto Rico; Goldmar; Nemagold.

soil   A light, sandy, not-too-fertile soil. This is the key, as too-fertile ground produces all top and no tubers, while too moist soil produces poor-quality tubers.

planting   *When:* As soon as the ground can be worked, early in the season.

How: Started shoots or slips are supplied by a few mail-order nurseries. Set out in rows 3–5 feet apart, with 12–15 inches between plants.

how it grows   The sweet potato is a sprawling morning glory that does not usually flower. The elongated tubers, high in starch content, are formed just below ground surface.

culture   Once planted, the vines are usually on their own, as too much fertilizer produces all tops. Weeding is important until the vines take hold and spread.

harvest   Dig the tubers when the foliage begins to yellow and mature. The skins are fragile and bruise easily. Store at just below room temperature, after curing for a few days.

pests   None of major importance.

diseases   None of major importance.

swiss chard

(Beta vulgaris cicla)

Swiss chard is a beet without an
edible fleshy root that has been
grown since ancient times.
Aristotle was fond of a red-leaved
chard, and Theophrastus
mentioned both a light green
and dark green variety. Cook
chard as a highly nutritious
spinach substitute.

where to grow	Chard can be grown in all parts of the country.
varieties	Rhubarb Chard, heavily curled leaves with red stalks; Lucullus; Fordhook Giant.
soil	Like beets, chard does best in a sandy, well-drained soil with a pH of about 6.5.
planting	Place seeds 4 to 6 inches apart in rows 18 inches apart. For good leaf growth, plants should be thinned to 6 inches apart. Succession sowing is not necessary, as the plants can be cut continually for all-summer crop.
how it grows	Chard produces heavily stalked leaves that are an excellent substitute for spinach in the summer months. They develop outwardly from a central-crown growing point.
culture	Water well in dry spells to promote continual leaf growth. Mulch heavily to keep weeds out.
harvest	2 months. When leaves have developed, the outer leaves are cut off about 2 inches above the soil to allow the smaller inner leaves to grow and develop. If heavily mulched over the winter months, chard will live over and start new growth in spring for early harvest.
pests	None.
diseases	None.

tomato

(Lycopersicon esculentum)

If gardeners could choose but one vegetable
to grow, no doubt it would be the tomato.
Once accustomed to the delectable flavor of
home-ripened, backyard tomatoes, supermarket tomatoes seem pale imitations.

Tomatoes traveled a long route from the
slopes of the Andes mountains, where wild
plants still sprawl, to the prehistoric gardens of
the Mexican Indians, who grew *tomatl* in their
corn (maize) patches. The migratory tribes
took their *tomatl* with them to North America,
where explorers from the Old World discovered the curiously fruited plant and took it
home with them. Although the Italians were
brave enough to grow and eat the tomato as
early as 1550, other Europeans grew it as a
curiosity, for the tomato was believed to be
poisonous (it belongs to the Nightshade
family). The French called the decorative plant
pomme d'amour, "love apple," and a poetic
Italian named it *pomo d'oro,* "golden apple,"
suggesting that there were yellow varieties
grown at that time. Thomas Jefferson grew the
tomato at Monticello, but there appears to be
no record of tomatoes being consumed by
Americans until 1812, when the influence of
French cuisine in New Orleans started the
tomato on its way to becoming a culinary
favorite.

where to grow Practically anywhere. The tomato is a warm-weather vegetable, being highly sensitive to cool and very hot weather. The newer dwarf cherry tomatoes are especially suited for growing in tubs and clay pots.

varieties Because tomatoes have become susceptible to many soil-borne diseases, the modern disease-resistant varieties should be selected whenever possible to avoid crop disappointment. As with any soil-borne plant diseases, rotation of the planting site is also important. (V = verticillium resistant; F = fusarium resistant; N = nematode resistant.)

Early: (all but the last-named early varieties are determinate in their growth habit, compact sprawlers, and not suited to staking.) Fireball; Springset (VF); New Yorker (V); Ace (VF); Spring Giant (VF); Moreton Hybrid (needs staking).

Main season: Heinz 1350 (VF); Jet Star (VF); Supersonic (VF); Ramapo (VF); VFN-8; Campbell 1327 (VF); Beefmaster (VFN).

Plum: Roma (VF).

Yellow: Caro-Red (F); Jubilee; Sunray.

Cherry: Presto; Small Fry (VFN); Tiny Tim; Patio (F).

soil Average garden soil will support a rewarding tomato harvest, but better results are assured if the soil is well prepared with rotted manures, compost, and high-potash fertilizers. Tomatoes are heavy feeders. Formulas such as 5-10-10 are good, or bone meal or ground rock phosphate. A basic cause of blossom-end rot is calcium deficiency. Where this disorder has been prevalent, lime the tomato soil at the rate of 5 pounds per 100 square feet. Ground-up eggshells are also good.

planting *When:* Tomatoes should not be planted outdoors until day and night temperatures are above 55 degrees. Low temperatures (below 55 degrees) prevent fruit set. Seed should be started indoors 6–8 weeks before the plants are set out, or use transplants, which are widely available. Plants 6–10 inches tall are ideal.

How: Set tomato plants deeply, up to the first leaves; roots will form along the stem under ground and strengthen the support for the plant. A lanky seedling can be planted on its side, to the first leaves. It will right itself in a day or so. Use a starter solution (half-rate water-soluble fertilizer) when setting out tomatoes to give them a good, quick start.

Nonstaking: Determinate plants (see How It Grows, below) can be allowed to sprawl on black plastic or thick straw mulch. Set plants 4 feet apart in each direction.

Staking: Staking is ideal for small gardens, and is recommended for the taller, indeterminate varieties (see How It Grows, below). Plants can be set as close as 2 feet apart in each direction; 3 feet may be better. Place the stake (2 x 2; 6 feet tall) before setting out the plant.

Tubs: Plant as for staking in containers that hold at least 2 gallons of soil per plant. A trellis or single stake can be used to support the plants.

Pole wire: For a row of several plants, 2 sturdy poles can be placed at the ends of the row and a strong, heavy wire attached to the top of the poles. Heavy twine is then tied to the wire above each plant, and pulled down and tied loosely to it. As the stem grows, wind the tomato plant around the twine for support.

Cage: To make wire cages cut 6-inch mesh concrete-reinforcing wire, which is 5 feet wide, into lengths of about 5½ feet each. Bend each length into a cylinder and fasten securely with wire. Cut off the bottom rung, set a cage over each individual tomato plant, and push the cage into the ground. The plant will grow up through the cage, and the fruits will be easy to pick.

Compost ring: Make a wire cage as described above (chicken wire may be more practical), and fill it with rotted manure, com-

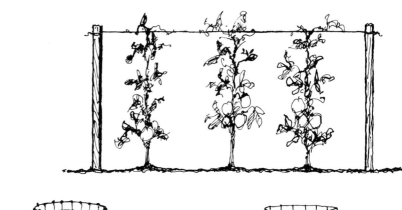

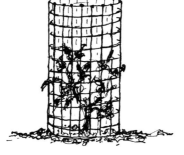

post, kitchen scraps, bone meal, and similar ingredients. Set 4 to 6 tomato plants in a circle outside the ring and stake them. As the compost cone in the center decomposes, keep adding to it, and keep it moist. The tomato roots will be nourished by the cone and produce excellent yields.

how it grows  The tomato is a vigorous plant, a heavy feeder, with attractive foliage resembling the potato, its cousin. The plants have a decided odor caused by gland hairs on the stems and leaves, which give off a strong-scented oil and stain when broken. The fruit is borne on spurs, which develop directly from the stem.

There are two types of tomato plants: The determinate, which are genetically controlled and whose terminal buds set fruit and stop the plant from growing (these "bush types" are usually early bearing and do not need staking); and the indeterminate, which are the later-maturing varieties that grow tall and usually need staking. The terminal shoot is pruned off when the plants reach the top of the 5- to 6-foot stake to stop their growth. These plants are also pruned of suckers, the side shoots that grow between the main stem and leaf axil. If not pruned, suckers make too much vegetative growth on the plant. Most gardeners prefer to prune their tomato plants to one or two main stems Plants must be tied to the stakes—they have no climbing tendrils—with soft twine, old nylon stockings, or rags. Make a figure eight with the tie, looping it around the stake and plant and tie loosely, or use a slip knot on the stake and use the free ends to tie the plant. Blossom drop is caused by cool weather (below 55 degrees); hot weather (daytime temperatures above 90, or above 75 at night), low soil moisture, and excess nitrogen fertilizer.

Sometimes hucksters promote the potomato or topato—grafts of potatoes and tomatoes. This horticultural fantasy was discussed long ago by Liberty Hyde Bailey, who noted in his *Hortus II*, "*Potomato:* A name once applied to the combination potato-tomato plant produced by grafting one on the other. The grafting can be performed either way, but the hope that by this means one can produce good crops of both potatoes and tomatoes on the same plant is fanciful, although both tubers and tomatoes may be produced if the potato is the stock."

culture Feed with a starter solution when the plants are first set out and again after the first flowers form. If the plants are well mulched, weeds should not be a problem. Water deeply weekly in dry spells. A generously moist growing season in the start followed by a severe drought period, will often initiate blossom-end rot, which appears first as a water-soaked mark and develops to a flat, dark leathery spot. It can be discouraged with mulching and consistent water levels.

Cherry

Yellow Pear

Italian

Pink Plum

Jubilee

Beefsteak

harvest 60 days (early varieties); 70–80 days (main season). Pick the fruit when it is red ripe, and check the plants every few days when the harvest starts coming. Store excess tomatoes in the refrigerator, but the flavor is best at room temperature. When frost threatens, pick remaining green tomatoes, wrap in newspaper, and keep in a moderately dark place. They will ripen gradually well past the harvest season.

pests *White fly:* Try to be alert to buying clean transplant stock. Use malathion for heavy populations.

Tomato hornworm: Handpick and destroy.

diseases *Wilts, blights:* Select disease-resistant varieties; rotate tomato soil.

Blossom-end rot: add calcium to the soil; keep plants watered and mulched.

turnip
(Brassica rapa)

This vegetable has a long, long history, and was believe
to have been cultivated by the Celtic tribes and the
early Germanic civilizations. It grew wild along the
Baltic Sea and spread throughout Europe as a popular
food. The leaves are nutritious as well, being rich
in Vitamin A. The turnip was first sown in the New
World by the French explorer Jacques Cartier in what is
now Canada. The root was also favored by colonists
in the Massachusetts Bay Colony in the early 1600s.

where to grow   Essentially a cool-weather vegetable, the turnip does not produce well where there are long, hot growing seasons.

varieties   Purple Top White Globe, the standard for many years; Purple Top Milan and Shogoin, especially for turnip greens; Just Right and Tokyo Cross (35–40 days).

soil   Average soil pH 6–6.5 will support a good turnip crop, but it can be greatly improved with an application of 5-10-5 fertilizer or ground rock phosphate along each side of the rows after the first thinning, since like all root crops, turnips respond to high phosphorus content in the soil.

planting   Germination in 6–7 days.

When: There is an old saw that says "On the twenty-fifth of July, sow your turnips wet or dry," which underscores them as a cool-season crop for fall. Seed can be sown in early spring, but the fall crop has better flavor. Some of the short-season varieties will bolt to seed if sown in spring.

How: In rows 12–15 inches apart, thin seedlings to 3–5 inches between plants; use the thinnings for greens.

how it grows   The turnip is a rapid-maturing root crop that has rough-textured, "hairy" foliage. The root tops will start to push out of the ground as they mature.

culture   Keep the rows weed free to keep the root developing normally.

harvest   45–60 days. Turnips are mature when 2 to 2½ inches in diameter; they deteriorate rapidly and become tough if they are left in the ground too long. The fall harvests have the best flavor. The tops are nutritious, and can be cooked as chard or spinach.

pests   *Aphids:* Grow nasturtiums near the turnips.

Cabbage maggot: Treat the soil with diazinon as the seedlings are thinned. Repeat in 2 weeks, if necessary, or use wood ash as a soil dust.

Flea beetles: Use rotenone or flour dust.

diseases   None of major concern.

herbs

"O mickle is the powerful grace that lies
In plants, herbs, stones and their true qualities,
For nought so vile that on the earth doth live
But to the earth some special good doth give"
                    Romeo and Juliet, Act II, Scene 3

Rare is the cook who does not add the subtle, complementary
flavor of at least one or two herbs to everything good to eat.
Although quantities of fine-quality dried herbs are readily available, there is a special thrill in being able to snip sprigs from the
garden to flavor dishes, or if there is enough space, to grow
quantities for home drying or freezing. There are ever so many
culinary herbs, with superb qualities admired even by Shake-
speare, but for brevity's sake the choices here have been limited
to a special dozen, which should stand the average homeowner-
gardener-cook in good stead.

Herbs grow best in a clay soil that is gritty, well limed, and friable. If too fertile, the plants grow lush and lose their flavor. A
sunny site is a must, as few herbs except mints will flourish in
shade. A dooryard patch is ideal for a few, or, if there is no garden
space, plant some in a pot, tub, or window box. Parsley, chives,
and basil, for example, thrive on kitchen window sills or in
large flower pots. Most herbs can be started from seed, although
transplants are readily available from garden centers. A few should
be started from cuttings.

basil

*(Ocimum
basilicum)*

An annual, easily started from seed,
basil grows as high as 2 feet tall.
The oval leaves are light green and
soft textured. Unless the plant is
pinched back, it becomes tall and leggy.
Snip leaves frequently to flavor
anything with tomatoes, or use with
fish and cheese dishes.

189

borage

(Borago officinalis)

An attractive annual herb with long
gray green leaves, borage has a
cucumberlike flavor that is excellent
in salads. It grows easily from
seed, and is an interesting ornamental
herb with its nodding, deep blue
flowers opening from pink buds.

chives
(Allium schoenoprasum)

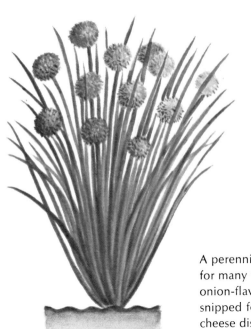

A perennial, that will remain in the garden for many years. It has hollow grasslike onion-flavored foliage that can be snipped for salads, soups, and egg and cheese dishes. This is one of the four *fines herbes*. Chive flowers are particularly beautiful—rounded globes of soft purple. Thick, overgrown clumps can be divided. Pots of chives are often sold in supermarkets during the winter months. Since these chives may be infested with onion root maggots, which cause them to fail in a short time, remove the young plants from the sandy soil, wash the roots carefully, and replant in fresh, sterilized soil. These pots will grow nicely on a sunny window sill.

dill

(Anethum graveolens)

Give this annual plant plenty of
room, as it grows tall (3–4 feet)
and wide, with delicate foliage
suggesting asparagus. The
feathery foliage is a fine com-
plement to fish, and the seeds,
left to mature, belong in every
jar of pickles. Although an annual,
dill reseeds itself readily, and
volunteer plants can be
encouraged to grow for the
following season.

marjoram
(Majorana hortensis)

One of the mints, marjoram can be grown as a perennial if protected over the winter months in harsh climates. The tiny, oval leaves cover the bushy, foot-high plant, and are often used with lamb, and beef and in sausages, as well as in stews and soups.

mints

(Mentha sp.*)*

There are many kinds of mints—
peppermint, spearmint, orange, apple,
and Corsican, to name just a few. They
are aggressive plants, spreading by
underground runners, and should be
confined by sinking edging strips or
bricks around their garden areas.
Perennials, they are grown from stem
cuttings or divisions and prefer
semishady damp areas; they fade out
in sunny sites. The mint flavors are
especially good complements to cool
summer drinks and to cooked
vegetables such as carrots and peas,
and they can be used in jellies
and desserts.

Peppermint

Spearmint

parsley

(Petroselinum crispum)

Primarily a garnish, or finely chopped and
used in salads, soups, and stews,
parsley is a beautiful plant that grows as a
biennial, living over to the next year. It
is grown from seed, which should be soaked
overnight before planting as it takes a
long time to germinate. The most common
parsley is the curly, dark green variety,
but just as flavorful is the Italian, or celery
leaved. Plants can be lifted and brought
indoors to grow in pots during the
winter months.

rosemary

(Rosmarinus officinalis)

In milder climates, rosemary is a handsome perennial, almost a shrub, with yewlike foliage. Often grown as a pot plant in colder climates and taken out to the patio for the summer, it is popular as a cool-room house plant. It is usually grown from cuttings. The leaves are most often used with lamb or pork, adding a distinct flavor.

sage
(Salvia officinalis)

Perhaps the most distinct scent of all belongs to sage, the fragrance from the foothills of the West. Grown as a scruffy perennial, it can be started readily from seed and thrives in poor soil. Sage and turkey stuffing are practically synonymous, and it is also an important ingredient of country sausage and other pork products.

savory

(Satureja sp.*)*

There are two kinds of savory;
summer, an annual, and winter, a
perennial. Both grow readily from seed,
or can easily be propagated with
rooted cuttings. Their rather peppery
flavor is a familiar part of bean or
pea dishes and they also do well with
eggs or in soups.

tarragon

(Artemisia dracunculus)

For the true French tarragon,
one of the *fines herbes,*
use either rooted cuttings or
root divisions; it cannot
be grown from seed. A
half-hardy perennial, it
is one of the most rewarding
herbs, as it thrives with
little care and can be
carried over in colder
climates with adequate
winter protection. Possibly
its two most popular uses
are in making vinegars and
in the dish Chicken
Tarragon. It is also good
with fish.

thyme

(Thymus vulgaris)

Although there are many kinds of thyme, the common form is the one grown for flavoring. A delightful plant with perky, tiny leaves, it is quite tough and will last for many years. It can be grown from seed or rooted cuttings. Thyme is excellent with ground beef and pork, and in soups and vegetable dishes.

growing
and
caring

stretching the growing season

The weather man has a way of cutting the growing season short with early frosts and late spring snows. But gardeners are becoming wiser; they are learning how to challenge the vagaries of weather and extend their weeks of harvest.

There are many aids in this quest, and short of a full-sized greenhouse, the chief one is a coldframe. This provides ample growing space for late fall and early spring crops, as well as room for starting seedlings in spring. The growing season can also be stretched with plastic row greenhouses and field hot caps.

The coldframe. The coldframe is simply a rectangular outdoor planting box with a window for a top and soil for a bottom. It is heated naturally by the sun or artificially with electric heating cables.

Most coldframes consist of a wooden frame fitted with a window sash top that may be raised and lowered. The frame should face south, with the back higher than the front, so the lid slopes, exposing the inside of the frame to as much sunlight as possible.

Coldframes are simple to make for those who are handy with tools—or even for those who aren't. Use whatever window sashes are available locally and fashion the coldframe box to fit them. You might even find old windows in your attic or cellar, or they may be available in junk yards. You can make either a single or double frame, depending on how much use it will have. A

A simple coldframe
can be constructed
along the south side
of the house to take
advantage of the sun's
warmth. High grade
plastic or glass may be
used as the covering.

Salad crops get a head
start in the coldframe.

double frame would provide space in spring for both crops and seedlings.

Most ready-made window sash is 2 × 4, 3 × 4, or 3 × 6 feet. The frame is easier to manage if it is not too large. Determine the height by how you plan to use it. For salad crops and seedlings, the frame does not need to be much more than 10 to 12 inches high in the back, with a front of about 6 to 8 inches. But some home gardeners may also like to use the frame to accommodate shrub cuttings and flowers, or to store a few pots of hardy bulbs for forcing indoors in early spring. Then the frame should be deeper.

Frames are usually constructed to rest on ground level. In colder climates, the frames are often sunk as much as a foot below ground level to provide further insulation. More specific plans for coldframe construction are available from the U.S. Government Printing Office, or local Cooperative Extension offices.

If the hammering and sawing and putting together are too much to contemplate, prefab aluminum coldframes are available from mail-order houses and from farm equipment suppliers. These rest on top of the ground and range in size from single frames (3 × 3½ feet) to double frames (3 × 7 feet) and have fiberglass lids. Heating cables can be ordered along with them. The whole package is shipped in parts, but is easily assembled.

The coldframe must have a southern or at least a southeastern exposure to be a success. This affords maximum sun during the day. Good sites are along a south garage or house wall, which will provide some wind shelter and access to water. Since the bottom of the coldframe is the ground, don't choose a site where the soil drains poorly, where heavy tree roots may cause problems, or where branches overhead will leaf out in spring and make shade.

When the site is selected, measure off the area to fit the frame and prepare the soil, almost as carefully as for spring planting in the vegetable garden. The soil should be 6 to 8 inches deep. Or the frame is filled with several inches of sand, cinders, or fine gravel. Seed is sown in starter trays and set on the sand. The unheated frame must rely on the sun's rays for warmth, and only the more rugged seedlings and crops can be grown—the cabbage family, leafy crops, and some root crops. (Tender melons, peppers, eggplants, tomatoes, and so forth need a warmer place.) Heat from the sun will be trapped under the coldframe lid and will warm the ground and provide ample warmth to grow salad crops weeks ahead of the normal planting season outdoors.

the hotbed

The coldframe's usefulness is even greater if some method of interior heat is used. This makes it possible to grow crops longer in fall and earlier in spring, as well as to start those more tender seedlings—melons, cucumbers, tomatoes, peppers, and eggplant. An old fashioned hotbed can be made by digging a 2½-foot pit and filling it with a fresh manure-straw mix and covering it with a 6- or 8-inch layer of soil. The fermenting manure-straw mix heats the frame and provides the warmth for growing plants.

The more popular method is the use of heating cables. The cables are relatively inexpensive, and come with complete installation instructions. They have low-intensity heat, around 3½ watts per lineal foot, and are thermostatically controlled; they will keep the soil temperature around 70 degrees.

There are almost as many ways to lay heating cables as there are designs for coldframes. Choice depends on the severity of the winters and the uses and construction of the coldframe itself.

Here is one scheme used in colder regions. A pit is dug about 18 inches deep and filled with 4 to 6 inches of fine gravel, cinders, or similar drainage-insulation material. Then a deep-sided coldframe is set in place. The cinders are packed well against the coldframe, and on top of this level layer 2 to 3 inches of straw or several thicknesses of newspaper are placed. This layer is covered with several inches of sand, and then the cables are laid on top in a rectangular grid, according to the manufacturer's instructions. When the wires are in place, the prepared planting soil is carefully filled in to ground level and the thermostat is set in the soil layer. This elaborate method of preparation allows extensive use of the coldframe, for growing both crops and seedlings. Plants and seed can be grown directly in the deep soil or seedling flats can be set on top of the heated soil. The ground is a good conductor and the heat will be uniform.

Once the coldframe is ready, it can be used almost year round. In the fall, hardy vegetables such as lettuce, radishes, endive, chives, parsley, corn salad, and roquette can be grown, making it possible to have fresh garden produce on the Thanksgiving table. In winter the frame can be filled with straw and used as a storage bin for squash, turnips, carrots, beets, and other root crops. Cover them well with straw for insulation, and cover the coldframe with a tarp or shading of some kind to keep the sun out.

In spring the same leafy crops can be started long before the normal planting season and seed of the hardier vegetables can be started.

Maintenance of the coldframe is simple, if you are alert. There are no temperature controls to open and close windows, as in a greenhouse. On days when the sun is bright and the sky clear, temperatures can rise at a rapid rate and ventilation will be important. A thermometer should be kept inside, even though there is a thermostat for the soil heating cables. A temperature somewhere between 50 and 60 degrees is adequate. If it rises above 70, ventilate.

For ventilation, make a small wooden sash opener notched at 1, 2, and 3 inches. Place it under the sash to permit some aeration, and regulate it according to the coolness of the air. Don't forget to take it out and close the sash before sundown.

On very warm days, it may be possible to open the sash of the coldframe completely for a brief time. If the sun's rays are too strong and the coldframe is overheating, then cover it with shading material—either lath or an old piece of snow fencing—or paint the glass with mud.

On very cold nights, the coldframe must be covered with old blankets, tarps, straw, or whatever cover is handy. Mound the cover around the sides, or stuff old blankets around the sides for extra insulation. If a late spring snow falls, brush the snow off the top. Although snow is an insulator, it does block the sun's rays.

Watering is also tricky and important in cold weather. Since spigots will be turned off, keep a gallon watering can handy. Water well and carefully to be sure the ground is moist but never soggy. If fertilizers are used, follow half-rate dilutions. Too damp soil may increase the liability of damping-off problems or rot, or both.

plastic greenhouses

Without space for a coldframe, and rather than give up any gardening during the late fall, winter, and spring months, many gardeners have experimented successfully with plastic greenhouses set up in the garden row. So many have had such marvelous success that their efforts are worth recommending.

The principle is similar to that of the coldframe. Plants are protected against cold winds and air temperatures, and trapped warmth from the sun keeps the soil from freezing and provides energy for growth.

The row greenhouses are made from lengths of heavy-weight clear (not black) polyethylene or cut from plastic painting dropcloths. Hoops of wire are made from straightened coat hangers or heavy-grade wire and bent into shapes resembling croquet wickets. These are then spaced out along the rows at 12- to 18-inch intervals. The plastic should be wide enough to stretch over the wire hoops with enough left over on both sides so it can be secured with bricks, boards, stones, or pipe. The effect is a plastic tunnel that can be left open at the ends for aeration, but that has enough overlap so the tunnel can be closed shut at night.

Though the air temperature outside may be quite frigid, enough heat is trapped under the plastic greenhouse to warm the soil and keep the plants from freezing. If the soil is well enriched with compost and manures, its heat-holding capacity is greatly enhanced and will help carry the plants through severe cold nights.

Even during prolonged periods of cloudiness, the row greenhouses seem to trap enough heat to sustain the plants. And if there is a succession of exceptionally warm days, the greenhouses can be lifted off for part of the day and replaced before sundown.

The major problem with these temporary greenhouses is securing them fast against high winds. They are so light that a good stiff breeze can easily pull them apart unless they are made secure. One recommendation is to tape the wire wickets to the plastic with heavy-duty tape to make them more secure. Commercial row greenhouses are also available with ready-shaped hoops, clips, and anchor wires.

The rows under the plastic greenhouses are planted in much the same way as at spring planting time. The crops

A plastic "tent" made of sheet polyethylene and looped over wire hoops will provide protected space for out of season vegetable crops.

Hot caps protect tender spring vegetables.

208

that do the best are salad greens—lettuce, spinach, chard, corn salad, roquette, cabbage, escarole, bok choy, and romaine. Root crops, including radishes, beets, and turnips, thrive too.

The rows should be planted in late fall, before really cold weather arrives, or in early spring, as soon as there is a break in the weather. To be sure that the ground is workable, keep a few rows well mulched with spoiled hay and/or compost so that the ground does not freeze. If the ground is hard and cold, place the row greenhouse over it for a few days before planting to allow the sun's rays to warm up the ground.

The row greenhouses will be easier to maintain if they are not too long. Two or three short rows are simpler to manage than one long row. To pick the crop, and water when necessary, the plastic is peeled off and laid aside, then put back in place and secured. The brief exposure to cool air (not below freezing) does not seem to affect the vegetables in any way.

hot caps

There is yet another way to circumvent the limits of weather and plant ahead of the regular season. Hot caps are inexpensive, commercially made caps of strong waxed paper molded in the form of little hats. They are turned up with a brim at the base so soil can be poured in to make them secure in high winds and heavy spring rains. These caps will protect such tender seedlings as melons, cucumbers, and even corn so that planting can be started several weeks ahead of schedule. Sometimes tremendous heat builds up under the hot caps, and unless watched and allowances made for ventilation on hot days, the young seedlings are scorched or killed. One way to avoid this problem is to cut a tiny slit in one side of the cap.

The hot caps come with a cardboard form to help set them in place. The caps are put directly over the hill after the seeds are planted or the transplants are set out, and the upturned brims are filled with soil to keep the caps in place. After the seeds germinate the little plants will grow rapidly in the trapped heat, and will often push up against the sides and tops of the caps. Break open the top of the cap to allow the plants to grow straight, or if the weather is settled, remove the cap and allow the plants to grow normally.

mulching

Nongardening friends often kid with gardening neighbors who make much ado about mulches. But let the friends joke; this curious word, both noun and verb, is one of the secrets of success in low-upkeep vegetable gardening and in building good soil.

A mulch is merely a covering over the soil to keep weeds out and moisture in. The word comes from Old English, *mylsc,* for "mellow" and Middle English, *molsh,* for "soft." These qualities describe a good mulch. It should be soft in texture and mellow to enrich the soil.

Mulches have many virtues. When put on a new garden shortly after the seeds germinate, they prevent weed growth by depriving them of sunlight. If weeds are not controlled, they compete aggressively with the vegetable plants for water, sunlight, growing space, and soil moisture.

Mulches have other virtues. They attract earthworms to the soil and provide nutrients as they decompose and work into the soil structure. One of their best features, however, is their insulation ability. They keep soil at relatively uniform temperatures, cool in summer and warm in winter. In fact, well-mulched soils tend to be cool in spring, so leftover winter mulching materials have to be pulled aside in the planting rows to allow the sun to warm the soil for planting.

This insulation ability also keeps soil warmer longer

211

Hay is an ideal mulch for vegetables, especially beans.

as the winter progresses, allowing harvesting of root crops well into November, in colder regions.

The insulation quality of mulch materials also reduces the evaporation of water from the soil surface. Soil that is cultivated and left unmulched and exposed to the sun's rays has a tendency to dry out more quickly and pack. When more moisture does reach unmulched soils, it may run off, where as the mulched surface permits slow percolation of the water downward. Also, there is less splashing of soil particles and less chance of disease spread.

The pluses for mulch layers on the vegetable garden are abundant, and well worth the small effort in laying them down. Once applied, the upkeep of the garden is greatly reduced. No more hoeing or danger of breaking off shallow roots, and any weeds that do pop up through the mulch can be pulled out easily. The vegetables will be cleaner at harvest time, and your shoes will be cleaner all season long.

how to apply

Mulches are easy to apply. They are spread between the rows after seeds have germinated or transplants are set out, being careful not to cover the plants but working the mulch carefully between them. The mulch layers must be thick enough to be effective. The smaller-grade mulches in low bulk—such as ground corncobs, sawdust, and wood chips—should be applied 2 to 3 inches thick. This will shade the soil enough to block sunlight and prevent weed growth. Spread the lighter mulches— spoiled hay, straw, salt hay—about 3 to 6 inches thick.

Before applying any mulch, be sure the garden is weeded, lightly cultivated, and moist. Mulch after rain or after watering to encourage moisture to stay in the soil.

what to use

The choice of materials for mulching is simply a matter of dollars and sense. Use what is available locally and the least costly. It is not worth buying mulch materials with fancy qualities or names simply because they sound interesting or may look attractive. The point is to use the simplest, cheapest mulch material available and use it generously.

Some regions of the country may have abundant supplies of a particular mulch material that is unavailable in others. Salt hay, for example, is probably unavailable in the Midwest, while redwood bark would be prohibitively expensive to ship to the East Coast.

There are two kinds of mulches—natural or organic mulches, which are biodegradable, and synthetic or inorganic mulches which do not decompose and must be removed after they serve their weed-inhibiting function.

organic mulches

bagasse Baled crushed sugar cane, a by-product of sugar manufacture, can be used for mulch where available. It has great water-holding capacity, and should be applied 2 to 3 inches thick.

bark chips The bark of coniferous trees, these are available in sizes from a small nugget to a finer grade. They make an attractive covering that permits ready penetration of rainwater.

buckwheat hulls A lightweight mulch, high in potash, with a warm brown color that is attractive and does not mat. This lasts for 1 to 2 years and does not decompose quickly. Spread at least 2 inches deep. More practical for ornamental planting, such as rose beds.

cocoa bean shells Similar in quality to buckwheat hulls, these have a decided chocolate odor, especially on a warm summer day, that some may find objectionable. The odor wears off in time. Spread at least 2 inches thick. More practical for ornamental shrub borders.

coffee grounds Used lightly, these can be quite effective. If applied too thickly without being worked into the soil, they mat and sour. Slightly acid, if used frequently add a dusting of lime to the soil where applied.

compost The most widely used mulch material, free for the making and highly beneficial to the soil. Spread at least 2 to 3 inches thick.

corncobs (ground) Ground to a rough texture, corncobs are an excellent, inexpensive mulch material that will eventually decay and add nutrients to the soil. Spread at least 3 inches thick. Because their decomposition requires nitrogen-consuming bacteria, add nitrogen fertilizers, such as cottonseed meal or ammonium sulfate, to the soil at the same time.

cornstalks (chopped)   If chopped, cornstalks can be used as a late mulch for fall crops, but nitrogen fertilizers must be added to control the nitrogen balance in the soil.

grass clippings   An excellent source of nitrogen, used in moderation. For best results, cultivate a layer of 1 or 2 inches into the top of the soil to initiate decomposition. Grass clippings left on the surface mat, cause a bad odor, and form an impenetrable blanket that blocks out rainfall.

leaves   Fall leaves are excellent soil improvers, but tend to blow and decompose slowly if not incorporated into a compost pile. They should be used as a light mulch; thick layers mat and block out rain. Leaves are handiest for mulch if put through a shredder.

manures   When there is an abundant supply, manures are sometimes used as top mulches. They are best worked into the soil at planting time, where they will do more good.

newspapers   An excellent, inexpensive, biodegradable mulch. Approximately 10 overlapping sheets can be put in thick layers, watered down, and weighted with rocks and soil. Though unattractive, newspapers can be covered lightly with other mulch materials to make the garden more appealing. They completely block weed growth. The question of lead leaching into the soil from the newsprint ink has been researched by soil scientists, and their findings show that only negligible amounts leach and there is little danger of contamination. However, glossy magazine paper printed with colored inks have high levels of lead and are not recommended for garden mulch.

peanut shells   Where available locally, these are lightweight and high in nitrogen. Apply 2 to 3 inches thick.

peat moss   Although it is attractive, this light, fluffy soil-improving product either mats or becomes too light and fluffy to be an effective mulch. It absorbs moisture much needed by the soil, depriving the soil. It is better as a soil improver worked into the ground during preparation for planting.

pine needles Usually recommended for acid-loving shrubbery, such as azaleas and rhododendrons (although they do not alter the soil pH), these can be used on the vegetable garden if in great surplus. Strawberry growers especially prefer them.

salt hay Where available, this is an excellent vegetable garden mulch that can be used for several years, as it decomposes slowly. Be sure the mulch is thick enough— 3 to 6 inches are needed to be effective. Excellent for melons, cucumbers, and unstaked tomatoes, to keep the fruit clean.

sawdust A fine garden mulch if placed thick enough— at least 2 inches. Because nitrogen-using bacteria must work to decompose this high-carbon mulch, add 1 or 2 cups of sodium nitrate or ammonium sulfate to each bushel of sawdust.

seaweed This has been used successfully on seaside gardens with neglible effect of leached salts. The materials are high in potash, and worked well into the soil, provide an excellent source of organic matter.

spoiled hay This is hay not fit for stock feed, and usually inexpensive (dealers like to dispose of it). Use as a mulch year round or spread after the garden has been planted. Apply at least 3 to 6 inches thick. Sometimes hay is a source of weeds to the vegetable garden, depending on when the hay fields were mowed.

straw Another excellent mulch material. As with the other high-carbon mulch materials, add nitrogen fertilizers to replace the nitrogen depletion caused by bacterial action.

tea leaves A fine mulch, high in nitrogen. Work lightly into the soil surface.

tobacco stems High in potash, these may do more harm than good, since they probably carry mosiac virus. Their nicotine content may have some insecticidal value, but may also affect soil bacteria and earthworms.

wood chips Where plentiful near mills, and so forth, these are an excellent mulch and can be used freely— but again watch out for nitrogen loss and compensate.

inorganic mulches

aluminum foil   Still in the realm of research, aluminum foil has shown some positive results in repelling aphids, which spread virus, on peppers, summer squash, and Chinese cabbage. The foil disorients their flight patterns. It may be expensive for large vegetable gardens, but worth a try if aphids are a problem. Remove after harvest.

stones, gravel   These are semipermanent mulches. They have some decorative quality but are not highly recommended for vegetable gardens, except for pot garden culture on patios and penthouses. They do keep the soil cool and moisture in.

black plastic mulch   This remarkable innovation in raising vegetables has proved to be a great labor saver and booster for larger and earlier crops. Although it is not especially attractive to see when laid out between garden rows, it is extremely effective.

Plastic mulch is particularly recommended for crops that have trailing plants with fruit on the ground—melons, cucumbers, squash, and tomatoes. It is also great for eggplants and peppers. Plastic keeps the fruit clean and overcomes the problem of weeds. The mulch is made of black polyethylene film (1½ mil), and is readily available at garden centers or from mail-order seed catalogs. It is sold in 3- and 4-foot widths and in rolls anywhere from 500 to 1,000 feet. (A clear, biodegradable plastic mulch is a possibility in the near future.)

Many questions arise from those who have never used plastic mulch, since it appears to be a smothering cover over the soil that would deter plant growth. But continual use of the plastic in field and garden testing has shown that the mulch controls weeds, raises the soil temperature, reduces loss of moisture, enhances bacterial activity in the soil, provides better aeration, reduces fertilizer leaching, and keeps the fruit clean. Plants grow faster, too. The fascinating reason for this is that mulch is impervious to carbon dioxide, an essential gas needed for the process of photosynthesis. High levels of carbon dioxide build up under the plastic, and it escapes through the planting holes, resulting in a high concentration of carbon dioxide around the base of the plants and boosting growth. Because the plastic absorbs the sun's heat readily and radiates it back faster at night, there is less

Black plastic mulch will keep vine crops such as melons and cucumbers clean. Stretch it flat over the prepared soil by anchoring one end with board and bricks (top left). It must be secured at either side with boards or soil to keep it from blowing away (top right). A hole for each seedling is cut in the plastic with an opened can (bottom left), and young seedlings are set directly into the planting hole.

frost injury than with plants mulched with natural materials.

The following procedure should be used when planting seedlings. The soil should be prepared carefully, in the usual manner for vegetable gardening, before the mulch is applied. Ideally, the best time to apply any mulch is after a good rain. Since the plastic is very light and easily carried by the wind, it must be laid on a calm, windless day. Anchor the mulch at one end of the vegetable row with rocks and soil and pull it lightly, but not taut, over the length of the row to be planted. Draw soil along the edges of the plastic to anchor it on both sides. The system works easily if two people work together, one to stretch the plastic and the other to cover the edges, using a hoe to mound soil. For best weed control, overlap the plastic when laying it down for another row.

Now for planting the seedling. Cut holes in the plastic, just large enough for the roots, using either a trowel, bulb planter, or opened can. Insert the plant into the soil through the hole in the plastic. Firm the roots well and settle in with a starter solution. Mound soil around the hole on top of the plastic so the wind doesn't catch it. Then in between each plant, on both sides of the row, cut a small slit in the plastic for penetration of rain.

The plants should grow along nicely without much attention. If rainfall is normal, enough moisture will penetrate down through the planting holes and rain slits to keep the plants well watered. However, in dry periods, get out the hose and allow water to trickle down into the planting holes.

If seeded crops, such as corn or onions, are to be mulched with plastic, the simplest scheme is to plant the seeds in the usual way, and after they germinate and the seedlings have grown to about 3 inches, lay the plastic between the rows just up to the seedlings' "necks."

When the final harvest is complete, the plastic can be saved for future years. Roll it up carefully on an old broom handle, tie fast, and store it in the garage. The plastic is not biodegradable so it will not decompose, and it should never be left on the soil over the winter.

composting

C ompost piles are the sacred rite of many, many gardeners who create their own special formulas and combinations of organic matter to produce what is so often referred to in garden circles as "black gold."

Composting is also one of the soundest ecological practices, for it returns plant and animal matter back to the soil in a highly beneficial form. The materials are piled up—the most practical place being right in a corner of the garden—where they remain for 6 months or so, until decomposed. Then this "black gold" is added to the soil to improve tilth, fertility, and ability to hold moisture.

Composting should be an aerobic decomposition process (well aerated) to avoid any offensive odors. The piles must be kept open and moist but not soggy, or anaerobic bacteria become populous and cause bad odors. A well-ventilated compost pile also decays more rapidly.

Compost is most economical if gardeners use available materials around the property to make it. Usually there is no need to go out and buy compost ingredients, though baled spoiled hay, for those who live in rural areas, is a favorite, easy-to-use material and usually not too expensive to buy. Basic items include autumn leaves, spent annual and vegetable plants, grass clippings, animal manures, and kitchen garbage. Never use meat scraps and fats, as they attract vermin.

One of the most consistently available ingredients for compost is kitchen waste—orange and grapefruit skins, lettuce trimmings, egg shells, beet tops, onion and potato peelings, among other things. A compost pile is an ideal way to dispose of such waste. Many gardeners simply keep a bale or two of hay next to the compost heap, dump the garbage on the heap, and cover it with a pitchfork full of hay. There is no odor, and within months even lobster shells are decomposed.

Because there is an abundance of compost materials available in fall, this is usually the best time to start the compost pile. If piled correctly and maintained properly with the right amounts of moisture, the decomposed "black gold" should be ready for use in the garden by late spring or early summer of the following year.

A superabundance of any one ingredient—autumn leaves or grass clippings, does not make the best compost. The secret to good compost is a generous mixture of several ingredients, each contributing its qualities to the whole. The mixture should be a blend of carbon-rich and nitrogen-rich ingredients to provide the decomposing bacteria with the right balance necessary for their function and yet keep the compost nutrient content beneficial. Most compost professionals recommend a mix of two-thirds carbonaceous material to one-third nitrogeneous material. Carbonaceous materials would include straw, spoiled hay, autumn leaves, wood chips, sawdust, chopped cornstalks, pine needles, and shredded newspaper. Nitrogenous materials include spent annual and vegetable plants, grass clippings, kitchen vegetable waste materials, weeds, manures (fresh or dried), and soil layers.

The chart on page 224 gives the nutrient content of common materials used in home compost. Meat scraps and fats should not be incorporated in compost, nor should diseased plant materials or those that might harbor overwintering insects, particularly rose foliage (black spot), peony (botrytis), iris (iris borer), and cabbage (club root).

There are two basic ways to build a compost pile— the Indore, or 6-month, method and the California, or quick (2 or 3 week), method. The Indore method (which was named for the state in central India where Sir Albert Howard, a British agronomist, perfected the process) is the most traditional, as it provides the homegardener a convenient way to use the fall garden clean-up materials in a profitable way.

The method is essentially a sandwich—layer upon layer of compost ingredients are piled up 4 to 5 feet. If these

An informal circular "cage" of heavy grade wire confines compost. It is easy to remove and replace when compost needs tending or turning.

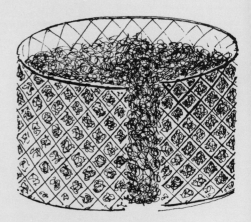

Compost Making

1 inch layer of soil

light sprinkling of manure, bone meal, or cottonseed meal

⅓ nitrogenous material

⅔ carbonaceous material

6 inches of twig litter

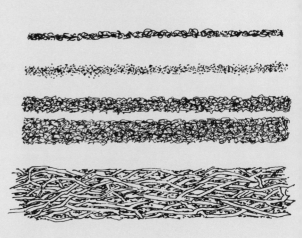

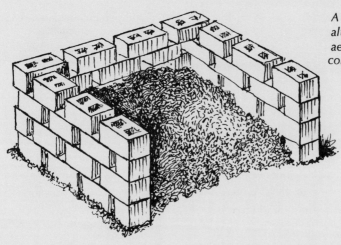

A cinder block square, with alternate spaces for proper aeration, will keep a compost pile tidy.

piles are turned over once or twice, they may decompose in 3 months, depending on the climate. Unturned compost will take about 6 to 8 months.

There is no strict size necessary for a good compost pile. Make it a size convenient to manage and suitable for the size of the property: 3 × 3, 4 × 4, 5 × 5 feet, whatever size is handy. The pile can be kept neat and tidy inside a chicken wire fence or cinder block square or left freestanding on its own. You may prefer it out of sight, though many gardeners find it most convenient to place the pile right in or near the garden.

The site should at least be on level ground and near a water supply so the pile can be wet down in a dry spell. Since aeration is essential to the compost decay, many like to pile a 6- to 8-inch layer of rough brush on the bottom. This is especially recommended if the pile will not be turned.

Another tip before piling: Autumn leaves, particularly maple leaves, have a tendency to mat and decompose poorly. If these are put through a shredder first their bulk is reduced and more surface area is exposed for decay. Or if no shredder is available, run the power mower over the fallen leaves a few times to break them up.

After you have assembled your plant materials, you are ready for the "sandwich making." On top of the twig litter, if used, pile about 6 inches of the plant material, keeping in mind the ratio of two-thirds carbonaceous material and one-third nitrogenous material. Add a light sprinkling of a high-nitrogen fertilizer—such as manure, bone meal, or cottonseed meal—and about an inch of soil. Damp down the layer. Repeat these layers until the pile is of convenient height, to 4 or 5 feet. It will reduce in bulk as it decomposes. To be sure the pile stays piled without tumbling, taper the sides inward, pyramid fashion, and leave a small depression in the center to catch rainwater.

The fast 2- to 3-week method for compost was developed by the University of California. It is essentially the same as the sandwich method, but all the raw ingredients are first put through a shredder. This gives them reduced bulk and greater surface area for quick action by the soil bacteria. Soon after the sandwich pile is made, it heats up rapidly, hastening decay. It must be turned in 2 to 3 days to keep it well aerated, and the turning should be

223

NUTRIENT CONTENT OF COMMON MATERIALS
USED IN HOME GARDEN COMPOST

Material	Percent (Dry Weight)		
	Nitrogen (N)	Phosphoric Oxide (P_2O_5)	Potash (K_2O)
Blood meal	10–14	1–5	—
Bone meal (steamed)	2.0	23	—
Coffee grounds	2.08	0.32	0.28
Cottonseed meal	6.6	2.0–3.0	1.0–2.0
Eggshells	1.19	0.38	0.14
Garbage	2.0–2.9	1.1–1.3	0.8–2.2
Grass clippings	2.41	—	—
Grass clippings / weeds	2.03	1.09	2.03
Leaves (freshly fallen)	0.5–1.0	0.10–0.15	0.4–0.7
Manure (dry)			
Horse	1.2	1.0	1.6
Cattle	2.0	1.0	2.0
Poultry	5.0	1.9	1.2
Salt marsh hay	1.10	0.25	0.75
Seaweed (dry)	1.68	0.75	4.93
Sewage sludge (digested)	2.00	1.5	0.18
Wood ash (unleached)	—	1.1–2.0	4.0–10.0

Reprinted from "The Biochemistry and Methodology of Composting" by Raymond C. Poincelot

Cottonseed meal and lime may be added to compost.

Layer upon layer, the ideal compost pile looks like a giant sandwich.

repeated every 3 to 4 days to keep the proper aeration and temperature. By the end of 2 to 3 weeks, the compost is ready for use.

Any compost is ready for use when it smells earthy and has a brown, rich humus look and feel. There may be some bulky undecomposed bits in it, and for this reason sieving through a ½-inch screen is helpful. Then the sifted bulk can be returned to the new compost pile. Compost can be added anywhere the ground is to be planted—to vegetable beds, flower borders, shrubbery borders, or wherever there is need. The compost is added simply by raking the material on in layers of 2- to 3-inch thickness and worked in. Once ready, the compost should be used, as it is not stable and does gradually disappear. When added consistently to the soil every year the soil becomes fluffy, easily workable, and fertile, and holds soil moisture extremely well. If you achieve this, your garden is sure to be the pride of the neighborhood.

When compost is used generously, there is an additional benefit—earthworms will appear in great numbers. (In fact, if compost piles are left unused too long, earthworms may be attracted to them in such numbers that the compost pile is reduced to nothing but earthworm castings.) Earthworm tunneling helps aeration, and their castings help to make soil more granular, especially topsoil. Earthworms also have some influence on nutrient availability.

weeds

Weeds are simply plants out of place. Many of them are beautiful and even edible, but when they invade the vegetable garden, they don't belong. They rob the soil of valuable moisture and nutrients that are needed by the vegetables. The 15 weeds shown here are some of the most common ones to appear. Learn to know them and eradicate them in their early stages lest they take over. If you know the weeds, there will be no danger of uprooting young vegetables or, like a young city couple was known to do—pulling up a valuable stand of asparagus.

Many weeds are annuals and survive from one year to the next by seeds. Pull these plants up when they are young, before they can flower and set seed. Biennial and perennial weeds are tougher as their roots will live through the winter months. All roots have to be pulled up to prevent their survival. Always remember that a good thick mulch is the first defense against weeds. The soil covering deprives young weeds of sunlight, their start to life.

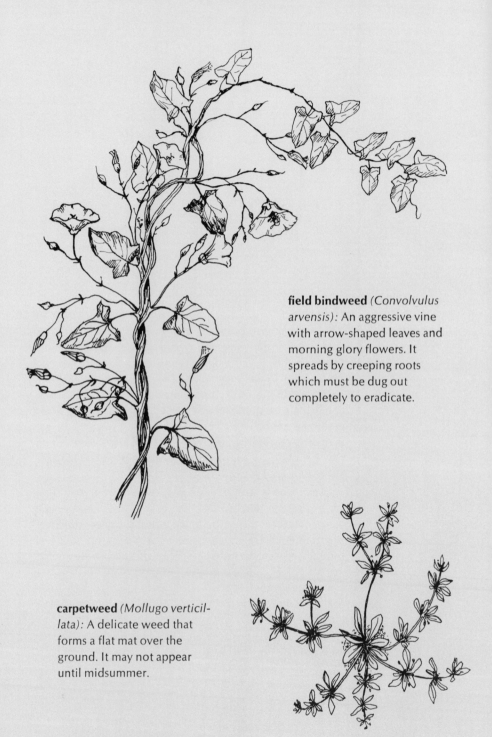

field bindweed *(Convolvulus arvensis):* An aggressive vine with arrow-shaped leaves and morning glory flowers. It spreads by creeping roots which must be dug out completely to eradicate.

carpetweed *(Mollugo verticillata):* A delicate weed that forms a flat mat over the ground. It may not appear until midsummer.

chickweed *(Stellaria media):* A rather attractive but rugged weed which displays minute daisies in the middle of winter. Easiest to eradicate in early spring when young and succulent.

galinsoga *(Galinsoga parviflora):* A very common nuisance, except along the Central Atlantic Coast, in damp areas and likely to invade gardens where there were once pasturelands and open fields.

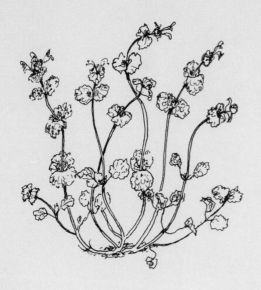

henbit *(Lamium amplexi-caule):* Many members of this family are attractive ground-covers, but this weedy form is a straggly biennial that can be persistent where the soil **is** fertile.

lambsquarters *(Chenopodium album):* Attractive, pale green, slightly toothed leaves, which some gardeners find tasty eating, make this weed distinctive. Eradicate it when small, as it becomes a tall lanky nuisance.

wild mustard *(Brassica arvensis):*
Many species of this plant are
serious pests in grain fields as well
as backyard vegetable gardens.
Though their yellow flowers are
beautiful to see in wild pasture-
land, the weed does not deserve
any garden space.

prostrate pigweed *(Amaran-*
thus blitoides): Thick, succulent, red tinted stems with
rounded leaves spread this
rather attractive plant over
cultivated ground. It thrives
particularly in open sunny
areas where the ground is not
too fertile.

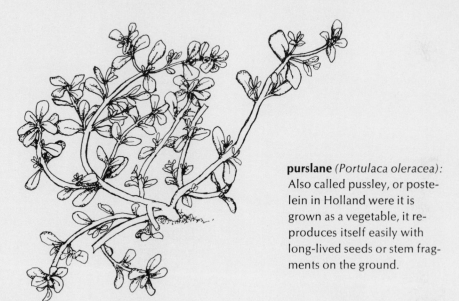

purslane *(Portulaca oleracea):*
Also called pussley, or poste-
lein in Holland were it is
grown as a vegetable, it re-
produces itself easily with
long-lived seeds or stem fragments on the ground.

red sorrel *(Rumex acetosella):*
Related to the edible sorrel,
the halberd shaped leaves
have a bitter taste. Their
appearance in gardens usually is a good indicator of low
soil fertility.

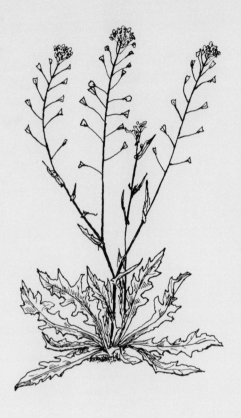

shepherds purse *(Capsella bursa-pastoris):* This is one of the most common weeds that will most likely invade any garden. The seed pods, which suggest a purse, are prolific and the seed is long lived. Eradicate when young to prevent reseeding.

marshpepper smartweed *(Polygonum hydropiper):* Long linear leaves topped with a tall, red spiky flower distinguish this nuisance plant which prefers damp areas and old meadowlands.

233

prostrate spurge *(Euphorbia supina):* A flat, ground hugging nuisance that is easy to eradicate when young, before it takes hold and spreads. Red-tinted stems prefer to crawl along dry, gravelly ground.

wild buckwheat *(Polygonum convulvulus):* Suggesting bindweed in aggressiveness, this nuisance has teeny white flowers along the stems.

common yellow wood-sorrel *(Oxalis stricta):* Though most of this weed's family are decorative house plants, this nuisance plant does not deserve space for its aggressive growing habits.

watering

Since vegetables are about 90 percent water, they must have plenty of soil moisture to grow. Water is also important because it enables plants to take up nutrients from the soil. Soil moisture dissolves the mineral nutrients so that roots can absorb them for utilization by the growing plant. Soils without moisture build up dangerous accumulations of harmful salts, rendering them useless.

Soil attains water naturally through rainfall or by irrigation either with the hose or by use of irrigation furrows between raised beds. (The latter is often recommended in highly alkaline soils where soil salts are a problem. The local Cooperative Extension Service will supply details on this kind of seedbed preparation.)

During a good soaking rainfall, the force of gravity pulls the water downward into the soil so that every pore space is filled. The soil is then thoroughly wetted to its "field capacity." This is the ideal, and the plants can grow without any soil moisture stress.

The plants will continue to absorb this available moisture through the roots (as pure water, H_2O) and gradually reduce what moisture is in the soil. Some soil moisture is also lost from the soil surface by the process of evaporation (one strong reason for using mulches, which help to prevent this.)

Unless soil moisture is added, the water will continue to disappear from the soil pores and plants may start to show stress and wilt. If the day is hot and windy, the wilting will be more rapid.

At this point, loss of soil moisture becomes critical and reaches what is called the "wilting coefficient" or "wilting point." When this point is reached, there is still some soil moisture left, but it is not available to plants. The plants must be rescued quickly with water from an outside source. For a successful vegetable garden, the water supply must be kept in between these two extremes during the growing year.

Water, either natural rainfall or irrigation water, has a tendency to flow downward in soils because of the gravitational pull. The better the soil structure—aggregates or large particles and generous pore space—the more easily the water will move into the soil.

Heavy clay soils often lose soil water because the tiny clay particles clog quickly and moisture runs off without penetrating. Sandy soils lose water rapidly through the large pore spaces.

Both clay and sandy soils can be improved in their ability to retain water if generous quantities of organic matter are added annually. In clay soils the organic matter glues together the small silt and clay particles to make larger soil aggregates and more pore space for water, while in sandy soils it fills in the big pore spaces and gives water something to hang on to so it remains.

There are two critical times when plants must have no moisture stress—when seed is germinating and when the crop is nearing its final stage to harvest. Watering is essential at these times, if not supplied naturally by rainfall. And whenever rainfall is lacking for a period of 10 days or more, get out the hose or watering can.

Garden soil should have an inch of water a week. The thinner sandy soils, which have poor moisture retention, require almost twice that much. In some parts of the country, rainfall does a pretty good job of meeting the moisture need, but in the Southwest and parts of California irrigation is necessary. (For details, the local office of Cooperative Extension can supply information on setting up irrigated garden plots.)

There are several ways to go about watering. The most water conserving system is a soil soaker, a long, canvas "noodle" that is attached to the garden hose. Water will seep through it into the soil with little runoff waste. A second resort is the sprinkler, which should be set up to provide the widest coverage with each sweep of the water pattern. Or an aluminum bubble device can be fastened to the end of the garden hose to break the water flow and permit it to trickle into the ground without eroding the soil. If one cannot be located, the hose can be turned on to a trickle so it seeps slowly in the ground, or a board can be placed at the end of the hose to spread the water flow and prevent erosion.

When to water? Any time. There is no harm in turning the sprinkler on the garden in the full brunt of the sun. The shower will cool down plant temperatures, and the water will not burn the plant leaves as some believe. There will, however, be some moisture wasted through evaporation if watering is done at high noon. If there is a choice, water the garden in the morning.

How much? This is the important question. Too little water—just a drink or a sprinkling—will encourage plants to develop shallow roots. During prolonged dry spells, these shallow roots become scorched and are often killed.

Average soil should be soaked deeply, at least 5 to 6 inches a week. This is about 1 inch of rainfall. Sandy soils require even more. Deep watering encourages deep roots that penetrate downward, roots that can search out deep soil moisture in between waterings. Deep-rooted plants grow better, and have more wind resistance.

How much watering is required to soak the ground the equivalent of 1 inch of rainfall? A lot. Northrup-King Seeds' research department worked out a formula. They say a 12 × 15-foot garden requires 120 gallons of water to equal 1 inch of rainfall. Since meters are rare attachments for garden hoses these days, the next best thing is an empty peanut butter jar or coffee can to measure the water. Place it on the ground in the center of the sprinkler pattern. When the jar or can is filled with about an inch and a half of water, turn off the sprinkler. Check the clock during this time. The next time you can water by the clock for that 1 inch of rainfall.

If all of this calculating is a bit much, use the finger-poke system. After the sprinkler, soil soaker, or trickling hose has been out and functioning for a time, poke your finger down into the soil. If the ground appears to be wet through well—and deeply, 6 inches—then the ground has had a good soaking until next time.

Be wary of short drinks or light sprinklings. They are almost more harm than any good.

what to do about bugs

There are probably millions of insects in and around suburbia, but no one has ever stopped to count. Besides, it's not that important. The insects go about their lives and we go about ours, and while occasionally our paths cross, it's usually just a passing glance. After all, insects have important things to do—supply menus for toads and birds, eat nuisance insects, pollinate flowers, build nests, and raise families.

But enter the vegetable garden and this serene live-and-let-live is finished. Casual tolerance becomes "do something to get rid of the beasties."

Time was when this "do something" was dashing for the nearest pesticide to spray away the creatures. Rachel Carson's shattering book, *Silent Spring,* changed all this and started us thinking. We are beginning to become aware that all is life—insects and gardeners included—and that what touches one, touches the other and all are interdependent. Ecologists call this the food chain; insects are near the bottom, gardeners are at the top.

Despite good gardening practices, vegetable gardens may attract insects. If the garden has bean plants or squash plants, bean beetles and squash bugs may find them. These crops are some of their favorite food.

A few holes in the cabbage leaves don't really matter, and a few potato bugs don't mean the end of the crop. And many times gardeners are satisfied to pick insects off by hand or tear off leaves on which colonies of bugs or their eggs are found. Handpicking works very well

238

with the gargantuan tomato hornworm, and alert hand-picking on bean leaves, where the orange egg masses appear, can keep the bean beetle population down. But gardeners are learning to tolerate slight insect visitations. If the six-legged critters do get out of hand, there are many devices, plans, and schemes for fending them off. These controls are presented here to provide as much help as possible. After all, the vegetable harvest is for the dinner table, not nature's half acre.

plant protectors

Some plants repel insects; others attract them. Gardeners are learning to understand these qualities in plants and use them to advantage as protecting "fences" around crops or as decoys. This planting is usually referred to as "companion planting." Information on this plant pest control is just beginning to be gathered by researchers, and many gardeners are adding to it as they learn more.

For those who would like to experiment and see how it works, here are a few of the current theories. The protecting plants are usually placed between the rows of the crops in danger or along the border edgings. Or, as in the case of some herbs, a few plants can be placed at the ends of short rows and still have a significant effect. The repellent plants will shoo away bugs while the decoys attract them and save the crop. The following list includes some of the best-known plants having the ability to repel or attract certain insects.

Garlic	repels Japanese beetles and discourages mice
Geranium (white)	draws Japanese beetles
Leeks	repels carrot fly
Marigolds	repels nematodes, bean beetles, and possibly Japanese beetles
Nasturtiums	attracts aphids or repels them (orange flowers)
Parsley	attracts beneficial lacewing flies
Pennyroyal (mint)	repels mosquitoes
Rosemary	repels Mexican bean beetle, cabbage moth
Tansy	repels many beetles
Thyme	repels cabbage worm

Another concept of companion planting was developed by the late Adolf Steiner, an Austrian philosopher and educator. His followers established a method of planting called Bio-Dynamics, a sort of astrology for gardeners, which is based upon the influences of living organisms upon each other. Their planting system depends on the effects exerted on plants by the earth and the cosmos. Several books on this method are included in the further reading list on page 277.

If the insect population appears to be getting out of control, more specific measures are necessary. There are two roads to take—botanical or kitchen sprays or chemical pesticides. All of the ones recommended in this book can be used with relative safety, and are not dangerous to the environment.

Pesticide is an umbrella term including acaricides (for mites); fungicides (for fungus-caused plant diseases); herbicides (for weed control); insecticides (for insect pest control); nematicides (for nematode control) and rodenticides (for rodent control).

Insecticides destroy pest populations either through the stomach in pests that actually chew (caterpillars, beetles) or on contact for those insects with sucking mouth parts (aphids, leafhoppers). The only correct way to use any kind of pesticide is to be aware of its potential and *read the directions carefully.* Safety begins with the user. Any pesticide labeled safe and nontoxic does not mean it may be used carelessly. Follow directions. Read labels, including the fine print.

Some pesticides are available in aerosol cans under assorted brand names. The brand name means very little; the active ingredient is the most important part of the printed matter. Identify the ingredient first, and if the can label does not list the one you specifically want, don't substitute anything else. Know what you buy.

Pesticides may be sold in dry (granular) form, to be used as dusts, as wettable powders, or as liquid emulsions, to be mixed with water as a spray dilution. Again know what you are buying, and follow the mixing directions. The materials will be applied with your own equipment, either a hand-pump pressure sprayer, a hose end for a larger garden, or a hand duster.

Spray materials should be used in the quieter hours of the day, either in mid-morning or late afternoon, never at high noon or when it is windy. And don't spray in the late part of the day, since leaves should not be wet overnight. Follow carefully directions on the number of days to allow between spray application and harvest.

the botanicals

The botanical pesticides are those made from plant derivatives. They are also called natural insecticides.

pyrethrum A contact insecticide made from dried flowers of the pyrethrum, a species of chrysanthemum, which is grown commercially in Africa. Pure pyrethrum has very low mammalian toxicity, but it is toxic to fish. Most aerosols have a chemical agent—piperonyl butoxide—to spur its effectiveness. Use as a spray for aphids, leafhoppers, red spider, caterpillars. There is a synthetic pyrethrum that is effective for whitefly, but this form is expensive and has not to date been cleared for use on vegetable crops.

rotenone A contact and stomach poison derived from the roots of two tropical plants, Derris and Lonchocarpus. It is low in mammalian toxicity but toxic to fish. Use as a 1 percent spray or dust. Use to control aphids, caterpillars, cabbage worm, and thrips.

ryania A contact and stomach poison made from the ground stem and root of ryania, a shrub that grows in Trinidad. Sold as a powder, it can be used as a dust, and it is sometimes mixed with water. Safe for mammals. Use for control of corn borers, squash bugs, aphids, and leafhoppers.

sabadilla A contact insecticide made from the seeds of a lilylike Mexican plant. It can be irritating to the eyes and respiratory tract, and it is toxic to fish. Sold as a wettable powder. Use for squash bugs, stink bugs, and harlequin bugs.

kitchen sprays

These are homemade sprays right out of the kitchen. All you need is a blender. There is no strict formula, but three different kinds of spray can be made—onion, garlic, and hot pepper.

Each is put into the blender with a small amount of

water to make a watery mush. This is then strained through cheesecloth, diluted in about 1 quart of water, and put in a hand sprayer. Sometimes it is helpful to add a bit of soap or dishwashing detergent as a wetting agent to help the spray adhere. These sprays can be used directly on all vegetable plants to ward off both sucking and chewing insects. Two or three applications every few days may be necessary for good results.

chemical pesticides

These two pesticides are included for use only if all else fails. They are both broad-spectrum phosphate insecticides with good records of safety. They are short lived and do a quick kill job of pests and dissipate without any chemical residue. Both pesticides are given favorable comment by the major national conservation organizations.

diazinon Recommended mainly for use as a soil drench to control cutworms, grubs, wireworms, and in-ground pests. Low mammalian toxicity, but toxic to fish, honey bees and some beneficial insects. It is sold in three formulas—liquid concentrate, granular dust, and aerosol.

malathion A general-purpose insecticide for wide garden use. Low mammalian toxicity, but harmful to bees, fish, and some beneficial insects. It is available as a 50 percent emulsion or a wettable powder. Use for aphids, ants, red spiders, mealybugs, mosquitoes, and sucking insects.

friends

ground beetle A rather ominous-looking black or iridescent beetle that moves quickly if discovered in its hiding place under a board or stone. It has strong legs and jaws to catch prey—chiefly other insects, caterpillars, and snails.

lacewing/aphid lion The adult is a beautiful little insect with light green gauzelike wings and shiny red-gold eyes. Eggs are laid individually on stalks attached to leaf surfaces. They hatch into ugly young called aphid lions with flat tapered bodies and strong jaws. The young feed on aphids, mites, thrips, and mealybugs.

lady bugs Gardeners often expect too much of this humble little beetle whose chief diet is aphids (perhaps

Ground beetle

Lacewing and
aphid lion larva

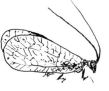

Lady bug and larva

242

Praying mantis

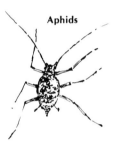

Aphids

Cabbage looper

Corn earworm

243

50 a day). They also eat scales and mealybugs. Imported lady bugs from distant regions often fly off or starve if there is not sufficient aphid population to feed them. Never destroy clusters of orange-red eggs laid by the adults.

praying mantis This grasshopper cousin is one of our best garden friends as it eats almost any insect, from tiny flies to large beetles. It holds its forelegs as if in prayer and catches its prey with lightning speed. Never destroy the walnut-sized papery brown egg cases seen on twiggy shrubs in fall and winter. In spring, they will break open to release possibly hundreds of teeny mantids. The young are cannibalistic and few actually reach adulthood.

foes

aphids Also known as plant lice, they suck juices from leaves causing them to be stunted, weak, and malformed. They excrete a sticky substance which attracts ants and they transmit virus diseases. Natural control: Lady bugs and aphid lion.

cabbage looper Sometimes called a measuring worm, it doubles up in a loop as it crawls forward. The worm feeds on all members of the cabbage family. Biological control: BT, a virus bacterium specific for lepidopterous pests. Or malathion.

Colorado potato beetle Often a serious nuisance. A yellow and black striped beetle that feeds especially on potato, eggplant, pepper, and tomato seedlings. Natural control: handpick; destroy leaves with orange-yellow egg masses. Or malathion.

corn earworm and European corn borer The green or brown earworm nibbles on silks, preventing pollination or eats its way into the ears and feeds on the kernels. Natural control: grow resistant corn varieties with tight husks or drop mineral oil on the silks (after pollination) and down into the young ears. The larger borer feeds inside the stalks and at the base of the ears. Natural control: Sanitation. Put harvested stalks through a chipper in fall to prevent borers from overwintering.

cucumber beetle Eastern species is striped; western species is spotted. They feed on young cucumbers, beans, melons, squash, and peas. Natural control: Starting these crops under hot caps to avoid early feeding.

cut worms Grey, brown, or black caterpillars of a night-flying moth. They remain in the soil and cut off young transplants above or just below ground level. Natural control: Use halves of milk cartons as collars around transplants when setting out. Collar should penetrate at least one inch below the ground and stand about two inches above.

Mexican bean beetle A copper-colored beetle about the size of a lady bug that thrives on all kinds of beans. Larvae are yellow flat creatures and feed on the under-sides of leaves until they resemble lace. Natural control: Hand pick; look for clusters of yellow-orange eggs on back sides of leaves, clip off and destroy.

slug (snail without a shell). This mollusk is a voracious feeder on most succulent plants. It leaves a mucous trail where it travels. Especially troublesome in damp weather, it feeds at night. Natural control: Ashes or sand where available or shallow saucers of beer, put out at dusk. Slugs crawl in and drown. Empty in the morning; repeat several times.

squash bug A brown bug that emits an odor if crushed. It thrives on squash, pumpkins, and melons by sucking the juices from leaves and causing plants to wilt. Natural control: Handpick and destroy leaves with red egg clusters. Place board on top of soil near plants to trap bugs; lift up in the morning and destroy them.

squash vine borer The larvae of a moth hatched in early summer. They tunnel into stems of pumpkins and squash causing them to wilt. Natural control: Delay planting of squash and pumpkins until midsummer. Or split one side of stem of infected plant with razor blade and puncture the borer. Mound up soil around the stem to induce rooting.

tomato hornworm A gargantuan, but beautiful green worm, it gobbles quantities of tomato foliage and some-times leaves of eggplant and pepper. Natural control: Handpick.

white fly A tough customer. A minute fly which popu-lates in masses and when leaves are touched, they fly off in clouds. They favor tomatoes and eggplant. A syn-

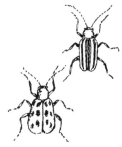

Striped cucumber beetl
Spotted cucumber beetle

Cut worm

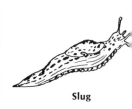

Slug

Squash bug

Squash vine borer

Tomato hornworm

White fly

thetic pyrethrum will control them but is not cleared for use on vegetable crops. Control: Buy high quality clean transplant stock as the white flies are troublesome in grower's greenhouses. Or use malathion.

nature's raiders

chipmunks Coffee ground mulch may help to discourage their visits.

deer Fencing is a sure protection or some of the newer repellent wildlife sprays are effective.

ground hogs Fencing (wire mesh or chicken wire) sunk below ground level discourages their tunneling. The part underground is bent at a right angle facing outward and sunk several inches below ground. Or spread a foot-wide moat of black plastic mulch around the outer perimeter of the fence. Ground hogs will not cross it.

moles Poke children's pinwheels into the entrances of their tunnels or along the runways. The vibrations will frighten them. Or get rid of the moles food, usually Japanese beetle grubs, by using milky spore disease biological control on the lawn. It is sold commercially as Doom or Japimedic.

rabbits Spread dried blood or moth balls around the perimeter of the garden. Or fill quart-size soda pop bottles half-full of water, sink them upright in the ground around the perimeter of the garden. The noise of wind over the top of the bottles frightens the bunnies.

raccoons They come especially at corn time. Wrap each ripening corn ear in a paper bag or sprinkle the silk with cayenne pepper. Play a transistor radio all night long. Or try flood lights on the corn patch at night.

245

diseases

Home gardens are not usually troubled in any major way by vegetable diseases. If plants are growing vigorously with good soil, adequate air circulation, and ample moisture and sunlight, they thrive right up to harvest time. A clean healthy garden is the best preventive. Healthy plants tend to resist disease.

When disease problems do strike, quite often the reason is poor cultivation practices. For example, growing tomatoes or cabbage in the same location for many years will encourage soil-borne fungus diseases such as verticillium and fusarium wilt on tomatoes and clubroot fungus on cabbage.

The simple remedy for this is crop rotation. Change the planting pattern and put the tomatoes and cabbage in a new place for a few years, or stop growing them for a year or so and try some different vegetables.

A plant disease will not sweep through the entire garden and touch every crop. Each disease has particular host plants. A cabbage bacteria, for example, will not attack carrots, nor will a bean mildew attack lettuce. And if a particular disease does appear, sometimes it may touch only a few plants in a row and the rest will remain untouched. In these cases the cure is very simple: pull up the badly affected plants and either burn them or haul them to the local dump.

As a precaution, do not compost the diseased plants. Disease spores and bacteria can live through the winter composting period and reinfect the soil when the compost is spread in spring. Though some claims are made that the inner heat buildup in compost decomposition activity is sufficient to destroy the disease infectors, to be on the safe side, destroy diseased plants.

The midsection of this book pinpoints some of the particular diseases to which specific vegetables are susceptible. Also, local newspaper garden columns, radio and TV garden shows, and Cooperative Extension Dial-A-Phone messages will call attention to particular local difficulties.

The best protection is prevention. Follow these basic rules:

1. Make sure the soil is well prepared, and enriched with nutrients to support good plant growth. Keep working on it. Remember that everything taken from the soil (harvest) must be returned to it for the next crop. Aim for rich, friable soil—the more care you give the soil, the better the crops.

2. Buy good quality seed and transplants. Vegetable breeders have developed many varieties with inbred disease resistance. Though they may be a bit more expensive, they are a bargain for trouble-free crop. Look for disease-resistant varieties particularly in tomatoes, cucumbers, melons, and beans. Both seed packets and seed catalogs identify these varieties.

Always buy quality seed. Don't save seed from your own garden even though it may seem fascinating and economical. Most modern varieties are hybrids and self infertile (would not set seed). Also, some diseases can be carried over in seed, so the better buy is fresh seed from commercial packets each year. Most vegetable seed is grown in arid regions in the western states where there are fewer disease problems. Also, many kinds of seed are pretreated for consumer protection with a mild fungicide such as Captan (no health hazard). The fungicide helps bean and pea seed germination in cold, wet soils, and protects corn from the seed maggot.

When buying transplants, be sure the stock is clean and vigorous, with strong stems and sturdy leaves. Examine the bottom sides of the leaves and look at the soil. Inexpensive, discounted seedlings may not really be a bargain but an unloading of poor-quality stock.

3. Be a clean gardener. Clean up weedy patches that may spread certain diseases and harbor such insects as leafhoppers and flea beetles. Some diseases can be spread by dirty tools, so be sure the tools are shining clean and in good working order. Don't smoke or handle tobacco when working around vegetables. The tobacco mosaic virus attacks members of the nightshade family (eggplant, tomatoes, peppers) and is spread by smoking tobacco. In fall do a thorough job of putting the garden away. Store stakes, clean tools, pull up and destroy diseased plants, compost spent healthy plants, and pull up and compost idle weeds.

4. Rotate crops. Change the garden planting layout frequently and alternate the location of the rows. Vary crops from year to year, if disease problems become serious.

5. Grow plants well. Keep them fed, watered, weeded, and flourishing. Visit the garden often and check the plants. Be on the lookout for anything out of the ordinary, and nip any troubles quickly before they take hold.

6. Don't jump to conclusions. Sometimes weather stresses—too much water or too little, too much heat or cold soils—can cause symptoms that might suggest disease. When the weather gets back on course, so do the crops. Never guess at disease diagnosis, or apply a fungicide just on a hunch. Learn to identify the diseases correctly and apply the proper recommended control. If a disease problem is suspected and it is a major onslaught, mail or take a sample plant to the local Cooperative Extension or State Experiment Station, or consult a local botanical garden with a query service or a reputable garden center. Any of these may be of some help. Well-trained professionals can quickly identify the disease and recommend the proper solution.

Plant diseases generally stem from three sources—virus, fungus spores, and bacteria. Virus diseases are parasites of live cells and are spread by insects (often aphids), mites, or nematodes. They can also be spread by grafting or rooting cuttings. General signs of virus are stunted growth, mottled leaf color (mosaic), and small or oddly crinkled foliage. The best controls are clean healthy plants and insect protection.

Bacteria diseases enter plants through cuts or wounds made by careless use of tools and through the plant's pores. They cause plants to develop spots, soft rots, and blights. The control is usually crop rotation or a soil drench, such as Diazinon, to kill the bacteria, or both.

Fungus diseases are caused by spore organisms that grow on plants to obtain food. They include mildews, which make powdery coatings on leaves, and anthracnose (from the Greek *anthrax*, "carbuncle"), which causes dead spots on foliage, smuts, blights, and rusts. Fungicide sprays such as maneb, zineb, and Karathane are used for their control.

penthouse, patio, and roof gardens

City gardeners with even the smallest terrace can, with advance planning, grow quite a selection of vegetables. Every inch of space can be used. Garden apartments and townhouses with small patios and decks can accommodate planters of vegetables to supply a remarkable harvest. Vegetables thrive in containers, and some of the most attractive vegetable gardens can be designed with interesting pots and tubs filled with an assorted array of vegetables. These portable gardens are fun to plan and develop, and the only limit to their size is the space available and the amount of sun. Six hours minimum is vital. More sunlight is even better.

The vegetables that grow best in tubs and pots are tomatoes, peppers, eggplant, and summer squash—zucchini and crookneck. All of these are attractive plants, and can even be substitutes for flowering plants and shrubs as a change of pace. Why not put tubs of tomatoes along the pool deck instead of the ordinary pots of geraniums?

Where there is a wall or support of some kind or trellis space, cucumbers and pole beans can be grown in tubs, too. And for large planters or deep window boxes in sun, leaf lettuce, radishes, beets, carrots, onions, and chard can be grown. For those who want to be more adventurous for a late fall harvest, there are the popular southern greens—mustard, kale, and miniature cabbage.

Seedsmen have taken the needs of the city-penthouse-terrace gardener to heart and made available an extraordinary selection of scaled-down vegetables especially suited to growing in tubs and pots. They are available from many mail-order houses, and are also sold in seed packets at garden stores in the spring. Though the plants are small and the fruit somewhat miniature in size, their quality is in no way diminished.

Here are the midget varieties to look for:

Beets: Spinel
Cabbage: Little Leaguer, Dwarf Modern, Baby Head.
Carrots: Little Finger, Baby Finger, Short 'n Sweet, Tiny Sweet.
Cucumbers: Patio Pik, Cherokee
Eggplant: Modern Midget, Golden Yellow
Tomatoes: Small Fry, Tiny Tim (cherry size); Patio, Pixie, Presto, Stokes Stakeless (2–3 inch fruit); Dwarf Champion (pink).

Seedsmen have also developed miniature corn varieties that produce 6-inch ears on 3-foot plants. These might be a novelty in a rooftop garden, especially if there are children in the family who want to see corn grown. The best miniature corn varieties are Golden Midget Hybrid, White Midget, and Midget Hybrid.

Often penthouse gardeners grow the full-sized corn and do harvest some crop. But for all practical purposes, corn is really a big space taker-upper and the meager harvest is not likely to be worth the effort. High winds will knock down corn quite easily. But suit yourselves— it would be a thrill to serve a few ears of city-grown corn at a dinner party, even if you only have one ear per guest!

Containers for growing vegetables can be anything strong enough to hold the soil and withstand frequent wetting and drying and the pressure of root growing. The most obvious containers are the handsome clay and ceramic patio pots, either domestic or imported from Mexico and Italy, sold at garden centers, craft shops, and potteries. They are expensive. So are the large-sized manufactured clay pots, which are becoming scarce as well. Even the pressed paper tubs and saucers are expensive in terms of substance and durability.

Wooden planting tubs, rice tubs, barrels, and packing crates are good planters, as are redwood and bark planters. Handcrafted wooden planters can be custom fashioned to fit along penthouse walls.

251

But just as serviceable, though not as fancy, are bushel and half-bushel baskets, gallon milk cartons, milk cases used to deliver milk containers to supermarkets, orange crates, wooden shipping cases, nursery tubs, plastic buckets, wholesale-sized metal food cans, and so forth. Just about anything durable will do, and part of the fun is using your imagination.

One essential to remember is that the containers must have drainage. Otherwise, the vegetables wallow in mud and the roots eventually rot. Cut holes in the bottom or in the sides near the bottom. Fragile containers such as bushel baskets and fruit crates should be lined with plastic garbage bags to make them more durable and to hold moisture. Don't forget to cut drainage slits in them!

One other tip about the containers. Penthouse surfaces absorb heat from the sun, and the bases of the plants can become very warm. Provide some aeration underneath by setting the pots, tubs and planters on bricks or heavy boards. This will also aid drainage. Also, litter and dirt will accumulate under these containers, and it is important to hose out underneath frequently. Ground-level patios don't accumulate the intense heat of the penthouse, and cooling risers may not be as essential.

Soil for containers should be lightweight, sterile to prevent weed and disease problems, and moisture retentive. The best answer is the packaged mix for starting seeds that is sold under many trade names. It is light in weight, and quantities can be used on penthouses and terraces with greater safety than ordinary soil, which is heavy, especially when wet, and expensive to have hauled up to penthouse level or carried into the city back yard.

Here is a recipe from the U.S. Department of Agriculture for making a large quantity of lightweight planter mix. It can be doubled or tripled if larger quantities are needed.

To 1 bushel each of vermiculite (horticultural grade) and shredded peat moss, add 1¼ cups of ground limestone, ½ cup of 20 percent superphosphate, and one cup of 5-10-5 fertilizer. Mix thoroughly. The nutrients will supply the vegetables for many weeks without supplemental feeding. When growth begins to slow down or the leaves begin to pale, it is time to start using water-soluble fertilizer.

The planting mixture is light and fluffy, and is easier

to handle if moistened a bit. If after this it is still not

A corner on the ter-
race has room for a
few salad crops.

workable, add some sand to give it some bulk weight.
Before filling any containers with the soil mix, check to
be sure the drainage holes are adequate and lay down
an inch or two of cinders, fine gravel, broken crock, bird-
cage gravel, kitty litter, or whatever might be handy for
drainage. If the drainage holes are large and the material
will sift through the holes, put several thicknesses of
newspaper on the bottom first. Paper is porous and will
not block drainage.

Fill the containers with the planting mixture, leaving
about a 2-inch space on the top to allow for watering.
The leafy crops and onions will grow very well in long,
shallow planters a minimum of 8 inches deep, while
beans and root crops—carrots, beets, and so forth—
need at least a 12-inch depth to grow well. Squash, peppers, and eggplant should have individual containers
at least 12 inches wide.

Planting does not differ much from in-the-ground planting. The same rules of hardiness and weather toughness
apply. The leafy crops like lettuce and the root crops
beets, carrots, and radishes may be planted as soon as
the air is warming and the weather is settling into spring.
A few cold snaps and light frosts will not be damaging.
Plant the seeds in tiny rows and cover lightly, and keep
the soil moist until the seed germinates. Use a light
sprinkler head on the hose or a watering can with a fine
rose head. The crops will probably have to be thinned,
although it is easier to control the seed in containers,
since the work space is in miniature.

Pole beans and cucumbers cannot be planted until
the weather is warm and settled. Tomatoes, peppers, and
eggplant cannot be put out until all danger of frost is
past. The tomato plants will need a stake to support
them when the fruit becomes thick and heavy. Both pole
beans and cucumbers will need a trellis of some kind for
support.

The rule for succession planting applies to penthouse
and patio gardens, too. Plan to keep the garden productive all summer long. Empty containers are neither attractive nor purposeful. At least three sowings of leaf
lettuce are possible, two of beets and carrots, and two
of squash. (One tub planted 3 weeks after the first.) Tomatoes, eggplant, and pole beans require the entire summer to grow.

255 Those who want to be especially adventurous can try

rhubarb as a container vegetable. However, it must have a large enough planter—bushel basket size at least—since it is a heavy feeder and a perennial. Rhubarb should be grown in soil enriched with well-rotted manure (the dried kind will do). It can be grown in the same manner as the other vegetables and has the same needs for watering and care. But since it is to live over the winter, it will have to be protected well to carry it through the cold season. Pack straw mulch underneath, around the sides, and on top of the planter and it should come through unscathed. Check the rhubarb several times during the winter, and water the ground if it appears to be dry.

Watering is very important with container plants. They cannot be forgotten, even for one day. If moisture is lacking, they will wilt quickly. Container plants need to be checked daily, twice a day in very hot weather. It may be necessary to water them in the morning and again in late afternoon. In very hot weather, hose the vegetable foliage in the morning. This cleans the foliage of city grime and soot and cools the leaves.

After the vegetables are established and growing the soil nutrients may be partially used up. This is the time to start using water-soluble plant fertilizers. Once every two weeks may be enough, though weekly may be better. You will have to be the judge. Overfeeding will cause lush green growth and sacrifice the development of fruit, especially with eggplant and peppers. Salad greens can be fed more frequently, since foliage requires high nitrogen. Weak, spindly foliage or mottled leaves may indicate hungry plants and a need for more frequent feeding.

On the other side of the moisture scale, too much rain can be harmful to container gardens. Although over-abundant rainfall is not a common problem, it has been known to happen, to the detriment of penthouse gardens, which can be literally washed out. If heavy rainfall is predicted, cover the planters as well as possible with plastic painter's dropcloths or old lightweight tarps. Or if there is room, drag some of the lightweight planters in under cover.

Since vegetables are annuals, there is no problem in trying to carry the crops through the winter with any kind of protection. But the planters, tubs, and boxes *will* need to be protected. Ceramic, clay, and plastic

256

planters will overwinter more safely if they are emptied and put under tarps to keep the snow, rain, and ice off. If the soil is left in the pots, it will continually freeze and thaw and in the process crack and break the pots. The soil should be kept in large plastic garbage pails. Wooden planters will store well with the soil left in them, and spring bulbs can then be planted for an early surprise of bloom. The bulbs will have bloomed by the time vegetables are planted.

Another plastic garbage pail will come in handy for compost. Cut 4 or 5 triangular holes at the base of this garbage pail for drainage as well as aeration to prevent the compost becoming odiferous. Balance the garbage pail on 3 or 4 bricks to add further aeration, and to keep it off the terrace floor.

Start the compost pile with a 4- to 6-inch layer of sterilized soil and gradually add to it weeds, faded flowers, spent vegetables, thinnings, and refuse from the kitchen such as potato peelings, egg shells, carrot skins, and fruit skins. Heavy skins such as orange and grapefruit will decompose faster if put through a blender first. Stir these into the soil and they will start to decompose. If compost is not decaying sufficiently when new material is added, put in more soil, add a handful of fertilizer such as cottonseed meal or bone meal, and perhaps some lime. The penthouse compost pile cannot be as well regulated as the country one, since the supply of organic matter is somewhat limited. But you can, while on strolls through the park, collect things like fallen tree leaves. The better the mix of organic material in the compost, the better will be its composition. Keep a child's toy rake or spade handy to stir the contents from time to time. And if the mixture appears to be drying out, sprinkle it with some water, but not too much or it will become a soggy mass. Terrarium moistness is about right. If managed well, this compost should be ready to use in 6 to 8 months.

growing
indoors

Those who live in apartments without a terrace, fire escape, or doorstoop can grow a few vegetables if, and it is a big if, the apartment has a southern exposure with a minimum of 5 or 6 hours of sunlight.

Then it is possible to grow dwarf tomatoes with cherry-sized fruit, leaf lettuce and maybe bibb, radishes, mini-beets and mini-carrots and possibly peppers. Peppers will do best if a friend can start a pot or two in their garden to give the plants a growing boost in full sun. Then the peppers can be brought into the apartment when they are flowering and the fruits should develop nicely.

Without abundant sunlight, indoor vegetables will not thrive. Leaf lettuce grows lank and spindly; radishes, carrots, and beets have skinny leaves; and tomatoes just kind of grow. If your apartment does not meet the sun requirement, you might try herbs, which do not require as much sunlight. An apartment with an east or west exposure and good light is suitable for windowsill herbs—chives, parsley, basil, and mint.

Apartment vegetable gardens are grown in individual pots. Minimum size for the dwarf tomatoes and peppers is an 8½-inch pot—a 9½ or 10½ is better. As clay pots become harder to find, especially in the large sizes, plastic pots may have to be substituted.

Or you can use your imagination for containers: try redwood tubs, wholesale food containers, painted and made attractive, rice tubs, or whatever is available. Those handy with tools can fashion wooden planter boxes for the root crops. Plastic windowsill planters can be used for the lettuce. One important thing: the containers must have drainage holes. If they are not there, make them, either on the bottom or near the base.

The planters will seep moisture, stain rugs, and cause ugly black marks on the floor unless there is some kind of protection. The simplest are plastic pot saucers. Aluminum pie tins, painted attractive colors, or heavy sheet plastic or old plastic table mats can also be used. Clay pot saucers should be avoided; they are not watertight, and there is some moisture seepage through them. Planters can be placed on large plastic trays filled with gravel, which catches runoff and provides some humidity. This sort of setup will also make watering easier. However, the pots should not sit in water.

Lightweight planting soils are simplest to use, and they hold moisture readily. The sterile seed-starting mixes are good and widely available in dime stores, garden shops, and many hardware stores. Or you may mix up a batch yourself, following the recipe on page 52. Unsterilized potting soil is not recommended because of the hazard of damping-off disease, which can kill seedlings overnight. Sterile potting soil may be used, but it is heavy and if many kinds of vegetables are to be grown, could also be too expensive.

Before putting any planting medium in the pots, place some broken crock or several layers of newspaper in the bottom to prevent the fine soil from seeping through the drainage holes.

In spring, transplants of the tiny dwarf tomatoes and peppers are widely available. The best varieties for apartments are Tiny Tim, Small Fry, Patio, Pixie Hybrid, and Stokes Stakeless. If transplants cannot be located, seed packets are available. Seed can be started indoors and the surplus plants shared with friends.

The other vegetables—radishes, beets, leaf lettuce, carrots—are started directly from seed. Sow the seed in a scattered pattern, one kind to each pot or planter, and pat it in gently on the top. (Don't cover the seed too deeply.) Water carefully with a fine-spout watering can, allowing the water to drip along the insides first and gradually work toward the center. Pots of vegetable seedlings cannot be watered as quickly or as casually as house plants, as the tiny seeds would be washed into puddles.

Keep the seeds moist until they germinate. It helps to cover the pots with a sheet of plastic for several days.

Once seed germinates, watering will be more frequent. Turn the pots occasionally to keep the seedlings growing straight, and if the tiny beets, carrots, radishes, and lettuce have come up too thickly, thin them to give them room to grow. Leaf lettuce thinnings are delicious in salads. Several pots of leaf lettuce can be started at monthly intervals to keep a fresh supply indoors all through the year.

Since there are no bees inside to pollinate the tomato and pepper flowers, you'll have to do it by hand. Keep a soft camel's hair brush handy, and as soon as the flowers open, check them to see when the pollen is soft and powdery. Then very gently touch the brush to the flowers and brush the other flowers with it. If this is too complicated, there are commercial hormone sprays available to encourage fruit setting. Buy them during the spring or summer months when they are in stock to be sure of having them through the year.

One tip: If plans for a winter vegetable garden are in the offing, be sure to buy the seed in spring or summer before the selection is gone. In fall, most seed houses are depleted of stock and the new year's mail-order packets will not be ready. Plan ahead.

herbs

Herbs are best started from plants in a windowsill garden, as seed takes too long to grow. Individual pots of chives, parsley, basil, and mint can be kept on windowsills in the kitchen for handy use. If these prove to be a success, then try thyme and summer savory. Herbs will grow best in a sandy soil mixture, the kind packaged for cacti and succulents.

Keep the herbs trimmed by using them frequently. This encourages them to grow, and prevents them from becoming lanky. Basil, especially, becomes leggy if not clipped frequently. The herbs should be kept slightly moist to the touch, but not soggy. And don't overfeed them. Once a month is enough.

sprouting

The recent popularity of natural foods and Chinese cooking has spawned the hobby of sprouting. Though not quite the same as picking vegetables, sprouting is fun to do and a form of growing your own. Sprouting can be done in an apartment with the poorest light, and all you need is a kitchen counter and some seeds. The seeds, which are sold at health food stores or can be ordered from seed houses, need to be kept warm and moist to sprout, and are ready to use in 3 to 4 days.

Many kinds of seeds can be used: legumes—lentils, mung beans, peas, soybeans, chick-peas; grains—rye and wheat; greens—cress and mustard. The sprouting changes the chemistry of the seeds, making them more nutritious than when they are eaten in seed form.

Sprouts are delicious in salads, soups, meat loafs, breads, and Chinese dishes, or when mixed with other vegetables. They have a nutty, crunchy flavor.

Lidded earthenware sprouters are available for under $12, complete with instructions and an assortment of seeds to sprout. They are sold in gourmet food stores, kitchen galleries, and some department stores. Or seeds can be sprouted in what is handy around the kitchen.

For easy sprouting use a large bowl, plastic colander, sieve, and towel. Like rice, seeds swell in volume after sprouting, so be cautious about quantities until you have gained some experience. One cup of mung beans will yield anywhere from 4 to 8 cups of sprouts, depending on how long they are allowed to grow.

To start the sprouting process, soak the seeds overnight in a large bowl in 3 or 4 times their volume of water. In the morning, drain in a sieve; the seeds will have started to swell already. Rinse them in cool water and pick out all the broken or brownish-looking seeds.

Put the seeds in the colander, place the colander in the bowl, and cover with the kitchen towel to keep the sprouting seed warm and dark. Rinse the seeds in the colander again that evening and cover with the towel. Repeat again, morning and night, a second and third day. The sprouts should then be ready. Store in a tight-lidded jar in the refrigerator.

Sprouts can also be started in covered casseroles, but these are more difficult to drain. They must be rinsed a minimum of two times a day to keep them well moistened and to prevent fermenting. Don't use metal containers or baking tins for sprouting.

More recently, sprouting jars have begun to appear on the market. These are mason jars, usually quart-sized, with a screen lid. After the seeds are soaked overnight, they are put into the jars and the screen lid is screwed on top. Several times a day the jar can be filled with water and drained to keep the seeds properly moist for sprouting.

Green sprouts are started in a different way. These are the sprouts grown for their leaves—cress, mustard, and alfalfa. Chia is stuffed into the grooves of the Mexican-made clay animals.

To grow the green sprouts, use a shallow glass or ceramic baking dish; again avoid metal. Line the bottom with several thicknesses of cheesecloth or paper towels and soak them well. Scatter the seeds on top and sprinkle them lightly with water. Cover the dish with a kitchen towel.

In a day or so, the seeds will sprout. Move the dish to the light to keep them growing and to green up the leaves, and keep the cheesecloth or paper toweling moist but not soggy. Start clipping the sprouts and using the greens when they are about 2 inches high. They are tasty in salads and cheese spreads or can be used as garnishes.

saving the surplus

One advantage of a big vegetable garden is surplus, extra crop that can be stored, frozen, or canned to feed the family off season. Winter prices for supermarket produce are mounting so high, the trend toward raising the family's year-round food supply may be an effective backlash to the rising cost of living.

Preservation of fresh food crops is economical for large families with big appetites, roomy kitchens to set up the production lines, and storage space for the processed jars and frozen packs. Freezing and canning, especially, require large kitchens with good work space, accessible stoves, and roomy sinks.

Small families may also find it practical to can or freeze the too-many beans, tomatoes, or squash that the garden produces and make pickles of the cucumbers. The following are some important things to know about storing, freezing, and canning. Before actually getting started, everyone should do thorough homework. Helpful books and bulletins to write for are listed in the book list on page 277.

storing

The key to storage of food is rescuing it before the killing frosts. F. M. R. Isenberg, professor of vegetable crops at Cornell University, has outlined some essentials on food storage, and with his permission, this information is given here.

For the longest possible storage, vegetables should be mature, be free of any diseases or insect damage, and be handled carefully so they are not bruised or cut. Otherwise they are susceptible to mold and bacterial decay.

One of the better ways to store small quantities of vegetables requiring cold or cool, moist conditions is to keep them in one of the older model household refrigerators without a freezing compartment and automatic defrosting. These units can usually be thermostatically regulated down to 33 degrees, and the amount of current required is relatively low since the door is not opened frequently. A cool location also reduces current usage.

For best storage, especially of root crops, wash the vegetables free of soil and put them into 2- to 4½-inch plastic bags with holes for ventilation. Close the bags with wire ties. Vegetables in plastic bags do not wilt as rapidly as those stored directly in the box. The relative humidity conditions are low in refrigerator boxes, as the moisture tends to freeze out on the coils, and since the plastic bags have a cold surface on which the water vapor inside the bag can condense, the internal atmosphere will retain a high relative humidity. The electric refrigerator can be used for either the cold or cool, moist storage conditions.

If no refrigerator is available or if more vegetables than the refrigerator can hold need to be stored, a box can be made from expanded polystyrene or similar plastic foam insulation materials. For insulation purposes, a 1-inch thickness of expanded polystyrene is equivalent to 4 inches of wood. A temporary box can be made from sheets alone, but any permanent box should have some light framing structure. The box should be located in a sheltered place, such as an enclosed porch, where it will keep cool but not be exposed to a continuous freezing atmosphere. If the box is relatively full, the vegetables may generate enough heat from their respiration to keep the box temperature above the freezing point. The box can be used for cold or cool, moist conditions, or for cool or warm, dry conditions, depending upon the location and temperature situation.

Vegetables can also be stored in outdoor pits or trenches, in outbuildings or cellars of outbuildings. Construction plans are available in USDA and Cooperative Extension bulletins.

Commodity	Tempera-ture	Relative humidity	Approximate length of storage	

Vegetables that require cold, moist conditions

Commodity	Temperature	Relative humidity	Approximate length of storage	
Asparagus	32–36 F	95 %	2–3	weeks
Beets, topped	32	95	3–5	months
Broccoli	32	95	10–14	days
Brussels sprouts	32	95	3–5	weeks
Cabbage, early	32	95	3–6	weeks
Cabbage, late	32	95	3–4	months
Cabbage, Chinese	32	95	1–2	months
Carrots, mature	32	95	4–5	months
Carrots, immature	32	95	4–6	weeks
Cauliflower	32	95	2–4	weeks
Celeriac	32	95	3–4	months
Celery	32	95	2–3	months
Collards	32	95	10–14	days
Corn, sweet	32	95	4–8	days
Endive, escarole	32	95	2–3	weeks
Kale	32	95	10–14	days
Leeks, green	32	95	1–3	months
Lettuce	32	95	2–3	weeks
Parsley	32	95	1–2	months
Parsnips	32	95	2–6	months
Peas, green	32	95	1–3	weeks
Potatoes, early	50	90	1–3	weeks
Potatoes, late	39	90	4–9	months
Radishes, spring	32	95	3–4	weeks
Radishes, winter	32	95	2–4	months
Rhubarb	32	95	2–4	weeks
Rutabagas	32	95	2–4	months
Spinach	32	95	10–14	days

Commodity	Tempera-ture	Relative humidity	Approximate length of storage	
Vegetables that require cool, moist conditions				
Beans, snap	40–50 F	95 %	7–10	days
Beans, lima	40	90	1–2	weeks
Cantaloupe	40	90	15	days
Cucumbers	45–50	95	10–14	days
Eggplant	45–50	90	1	week
Peppers, sweet	45–50	95	2–3	weeks
Potatoes, early	50	90	1–3	weeks
Potatoes, late	40	90	4–9	months
Tomatoes, green	50–70	90	1–3	weeks
Tomatoes, ripe	45–50	90	4–7	days
Watermelon	40–50	80–85	2–3	weeks
Vegetables that require cool, dry conditions				
Garlic	32	65–70	6–7	months
Onions, dry	32	65–70	6–7	months
Vegetables that require warm, dry conditions				
Peppers, chili, dry	50	60–65	6	months
Pumpkins	50–55	70–75	2–3	months
Squash, winter	50–55	50–60	2–6	months
Sweet potato	55–60	80–85	4–6	months

Vegetables for storage are grouped according to their temperature and humidity requirements. The maximum storage conditions that a homeowner can usually achieve are cold, moist conditions; cool, moist conditions; cool, dry conditions; or warm, dry conditions.

Temperature and humidity requirements for most vegetables are listed in the table, prepared by Professor Isenberg.

The most useful, trouble-free instrument for estimating the temperature/humidity levels for stored vegetables is the Mason or Taylor wall-type hygrometer (psychometer). These instruments have two matched thermometers, the bulb of one of which is covered with a woven, wettable sock. The sock is wetted with water, preferably distilled, and allowed to adjust to the humidity of the storage. Usually it will show a lower temperature reading than the dry bulb. Relative humidity can be determined from a set of tables based on the differences in degrees between the two thermometer readings.

freezing

Only high-quality vegetables in their prime are suitable for freezing. It is useless to freeze half-ripe, overripe, or tasteless vegetables. The crop should be firm, fully ripe, and freshly picked, free of insect damage and disease. The crops captured at their flavorful best, will freeze well and results will be worthwhile and delicious to eat.

Soils, climates, growing conditions, and local variety preferences make wide differences in the quality of harvest and its suitability for freezing. One variety that may grow, and therefore freeze, well in a particular locale may not grow as favorably in another. For this reason, check with the local Cooperative Extension or state extension at the university for the varieties recommended for freezing and canning.

Foods destined for the freezer must be blanched or scalded in rapidly boiling water. This process insures the high quality for the vegetables in the frozen pack. Blanching slows down the growing of bacteria, molds, and yeasts and retards enzymes in the vegetable, stopping it at its peak of perfection and good ripe color. If the vegetable is not heated properly before freezing, this activity proceeds unchecked, and can cause off-flavor or discoloration in the frozen product.

After blanching, the vegetables are cooled down quickly in ice-cold water to stop their cooking. As soon as they are thoroughly chilled, they are packed and sealed. The scalding times vary for each vegetable; many cookbooks as well as guides on freezing provide blanching and cooling time charts.

The following vegetables freeze especially well:

Asparagus	Corn	Pumpkin (puree)
Beans	Eggplant	Rutabaga
Beets	Mushrooms	Spinach
Broccoli	Okra	Squash (mashed)
Brussels sprouts	Peas	Tomatoes (stewed)
Carrots	Peppers	Turnips
Cauliflower	Potatoes	

canning

As in freezing, vegetables for canning must be picked at their peak of perfection for good flavor and color. Wash them thoroughly and discard any that are diseased or badly damaged by insects. The essential principle of canning is heating vegetables hot enough and long enough to destroy the microorganisms that cause food spoilage—molds, yeast, and bacteria. The jars, too, must be sterile, clean, free of crack, and have lids in good condition for tight seals.

There are two processes for canning, pressure and boiling water bath. All low-acid vegetables—beans, beets, corn, and so forth—must be pressure processed at 240 degrees, while acid foods—pickled vegetables, fruits, relishes, and tomatoes—are processed in a boiling water bath (212 degrees). The steam-pressure canner can attain the higher temperatures required for processing safely. Process directions are provided with this equipment. Follow them carefully, and keep the equipment clean and in good working order. Never store jars without checking 24 hours later to see that the seals are tight and proper. Press the flat metal lid. If it does not move, the seal is tight. Tap the lid with a spoon; a clear ring means a good seal. Never taste any questionable looking jar to see if it is safe to eat. Off color, broken seals with bulging jar rings spurting liquid and gas bubbles are clearly danger signs, as are mold and odor.

All low-acid home-canned foods should be boiled for

268

15 minutes before eating. If the liquid foams or has an unnatural odor when heated, the vegetable is spoiled and should be thrown out immediately.

If directions are followed carefully and the equipment is in good safe working order, many delicious and fascinating relishes and vegetable and fruit combinations can be stashed away for winter. Who would ever pass up Mom's delicious relishes or homemade pickles? The following vegetables also can readily:

Asparagus	Eggplant	Spinach
Beans	Okra	Squash
Beets	Peas	Tomatoes
Carrots	Peppers	
Corn	Potatoes	

when winter comes

The vegetable garden has a natural way of winding down at the end of the season. The days become shorter, the sun's rays lower, and it takes just a bit longer for the last tomatoes to ripen and the remaining few ears of corn to mature, while the pumpkins and squash lie ready for harvest.

Another sign that the garden season is coming to an end is a frost warning on the radio or TV weather broadcast. This sudden invasion by Mother Nature abruptly puts gardeners on notice that the idyllic days of being outdoors tending crops are drawing short. And emergency measures should be taken.

If the frost is just a light frost, sometimes even the tenderest vegetables sneak through, especially if the garden is on a slope. Frost hits the high spots and rolls down into the deep, low valleys, where it settles.

The tenderest vegetables marked for destruction by the first *heavy* frost are tomatoes, eggplant, cucumbers, peppers, melons, and summer squash. Frost blackens them overnight, and that is the end. As a precaution when the frost prediction comes, harvest any fruits both ripe and unripe left on these plants. Trying to cover the plants is useless for, even if blanketed and protected, once they have been chilled down by cold temperature, the remaining fruits on the plants never ripen to a satisfactory flavor. Store rescued fruits in any airy, warm room indoors where they will ripen. Quickly can or freeze ripe surplus before it loses its good flavor.

270

Leaf lettuce and head lettuce will sneak through light frosts. Cover them with newspaper "tents" as added safety.

A few vegetables are improved by frosts: parsnips, kale, salsify, and perhaps spinach. The cabbage family, in general, is frost tough, and most of these cousins—cabbage, broccoli, cauliflower, and Brussels sprouts—will go through several frosts unharmed.

As soon as frost has hit the garden, the blackened plants should be pulled up, and most of them added to the compost pile. If stakes were used for tomatoes and trellises for the cucumbers, pull these up, too. Brush off the dirt and store them in the garage or tool shed.

Spent vegetable plants can be tossed safely on the compost pile except for two—corn stalks and badly diseased plants. Corn stalks are winter havens for the corn borer, and composting whole stalks only provides this nuisance with a safe winter home. The corn stalks should be put through a chipper, and then they can be safely composted or spread on the garden as a winter mulch. Badly diseased plant tops should be hauled away to the town dump, or if the town ordinance permits burning, burned.

The actual closing of the garden can be done in several ways; choice is left to the family's plans and involvement.

For those who have a summer home and leave the house in late fall, not to see it again until spring, the closing is simple.

Home-away-from-home gardens are ideal left open and covered with compost material—spent vegetable tops, the mulches from the summer, any spoiled hay that might be available, and some accumulation of fall leaves.

If the summer house is located in a region where spring is late and the soil dries out slowly, fall plowing-in of this top composting will hasten spring planting. The following spring, only stiff raking and an addition of fertilizer will be needed to start the spring season. Otherwise, the top winter mulch material can stay in place until spring, when the family returns, and can be plowed under then.

For those who don't have to leave their gardens, sheet composting, a variation on the top winter mulch, is a good solution. This type of composting is an "in-place" compost pile of mulch materials right on the garden, added to all through the winter months (except when there is very deep snow). The method will accommodate kitchen wastes such as potato peelings, egg shells, orange and other fruit skins, lettuce tops, carrot peelings, and so forth. Add the kitchen wastes to the compost, cover them, and they will start to decompose without odor. No meats, of course, should ever be added. This top compost is dug into the vegetable garden in spring before planting.

Another possibility is thick layers of straw or spoiled hay spread on top of the garden in late summer, when the crops have been fully harvested, and rototilled into the soil. This practice will allow the nitrogen-consuming bacteria time to work on the high-carbonaceous straw and hay without depleting crops of their natural nitrogen supply. By spring, the straw or hay will be fairly well decomposed and the nitrogen balance restored.

Green manure covers can be planted in the vegetable garden in late summer. They will grow partially in fall, and are dug under in spring before the planting season. These crops supply much-needed organic matter to badly depleted soils, and are recommended where there is great need for soil improvement. Green manure crops are rye, vetch, soybeans or clover. These seeds can be broadcast openly over the soil or planted in the rows after each vegetable crop has been harvested.

Don't forget to clean and polish all tools before putting them away. And as a final gesture to the tucking-in process, review the garden and its crops and your tending of them. Make notes on what went well and where there is room for improvement. For in not too many months the seed catalogs will be arriving, and that excitement of planning will begin all over again.

where to
get help

publications

The United States Government Printing Office publishes a wide range of pamphlets and bulletins on garden and agricultural subjects. They are available for nominal sums to anyone who orders them. Because of the enormity of mail requests for government publications, orders seem to take a long time in coming. Be patient! A list of publications on gardening may be ordered from:

Superintendent of Documents
Government Printing Office
Washington, D.C. 20402

cooperative extension

The national system of Cooperative Extension is a service-oriented program linked with each state's agricultural (land-grant) college and the U.S. Department of Agriculture. Almost every county in the nation has an office of Cooperative Extension located in its county seat. They service agriculture, home horticulture, 4-H, and home economics programs with knowledge, guidance, and help.

These offices are listed in phone books, usually under the county government, and the staff members who service the agriculture–horticulture program are called County Agents. Homeowners can telephone them for information, order bulletins and pamphlets on gardening published by the state's land-grant college, send samples for soil testing, or visit the offices personally for identification of specific garden problems. Many of these offices in large metropolitan regions have public field days and planting demonstrations.

Headquarters for each state's Cooperative Extension network are in the state's agricultural college or university. Bulletins and pamphlets may also be ordered directly from these schools by state residents. Most of them are free, or costs are nominal.

alabama
Cooperative Extension Service
Auburn University
Auburn 36830

arizona
Cooperative Extension Service
University of Arizona
College of Agriculture
Tucson 85721

arkansas
Cooperative Extension Service
University of Arkansas
P. O. Box 391
Little Rock 72203

california
Agricultural Extension Service
University of California
College of Agriculture
Berkeley 94720

colorado
Cooperative Extension Service
Colorado State University
Fort Collins 80521

connecticut
Cooperative Extension Service
University of Connecticut
College of Agriculture and
   Natural Resources
Storrs 06268

delaware
Cooperative Extension Service
University of Delaware
College of Agricultural Sciences
Newark 19711

district of columbia
Cooperative Extension Service
The Federal City College
1424 K Street, N.W.
Washington, D.C. 20005

florida
Cooperative Extension Service
University of Florida
Institute of Food and
   Agricultural Sciences
Gainesville 32601

georgia
Cooperative Extension Service
University of Georgia
College of Agriculture
Athens 30601

idaho
Cooperative Extension Service
University of Idaho
College of Agriculture
Moscow 83843

illinois
Cooperative Extension Service
University of Illinois
College of Agriculture
Urbana 61801

indiana
Cooperative Extension Service
Purdue University
West Lafayette 47907

iowa
Cooperative Extension Service
Iowa State University
Ames 50010

kansas
Cooperative Extension Service
Kansas State University
Manhattan 66506

kentucky
Cooperative Extension Service
University of Kentucky
College of Agriculture
Lexington 40506

louisiana
Cooperative Extension Service
State University
A & M College
University Station
Baton Rouge 70803

maine
Cooperative Extension Service
University of Maine
Orono 04473

maryland
Cooperative Extension Service
University of Maryland
College Park 20742

274

massachusetts
Cooperative Extension Service
University of Massachusetts
Amherst 01002

michigan
Cooperative Extension Service
Michigan State University
East Lansing 48823

minnesota
Agricultural Extension Service
University of Minnesota
Institute of Agriculture
St. Paul 55101

mississippi
Cooperative Extension Service
Mississippi State University
State College 39762

missouri
Cooperative Extension Service
University of Missouri
Columbia 65201

montana
Cooperative Extension Service
Montana State University
Bozeman 59715

nebraska
Cooperative Extension Service
University of Nebraska
College of Agriculture
and Home Economics
Lincoln 68503

nevada
Cooperative Extension Service
University of Nevada
College of Agriculture
Reno 89507

new hampshire
Cooperative Extension Service
University of New Hampshire
College of Life Sciences
and Agriculture
Durham 03824

new jersey
Cooperative Extension Service
College of Agriculture
and Environmental Science
Rutgers—The State University
New Brunswick 08903

new mexico
Cooperative Extension Service
New Mexico State University
Box 3AE, Agriculture Bldg.
Las Cruces 88003

new york
Cooperative Extension Service
Cornell University
State University of New York
Ithaca 14850

north carolina
Cooperative Extension Service
North Carolina State University
P.O. Box 5157
Raleigh 27607

north dakota
Cooperative Extension Service
North Dakota State University
of Agriculture and Applied Science
University Station
Fargo 58102

ohio
Cooperative Extension Service
Ohio State University
Agriculture Administration Bldg.
2120 Fyffe Road
Columbus 43210

oklahoma
Cooperative Extension Service
Oklahoma State University
201 Whitehurst
Stillwater 74074

oregon
Cooperative Extension Service
Oregon State University
Corvallis 97331

pennsylvania
Cooperative Extension Service
The Pennsylvania State University
College of Agriculture
323 Agricultural Administration Bldg.
University Park 16802

rhode island
Cooperative Extension Service
University of Rhode Island
Kingston 02881

south carolina
Cooperative Extension Service
Clemson University
Clemson 29631

south dakota
Cooperative Extension Service
South Dakota State University
College of Agriculture
Brookings 57006

tennessee
Agricultural Extension Service
University of Tennessee
Institute of Agriculture
P.O. Box 1071
Knoxville 37901

texas
Agricultural Extension Service
Texas A & M University
College Station 77843

utah
Cooperative Extension Service
Utah State University
Logan 84321

vermont
Cooperative Extension Service
University of Vermont
Burlington 05401

virginia
Cooperative Extension Service
Virginia Polytechnic Institute
Blacksburg 24061

washington
Cooperative Extension Service
Washington State University
College of Agriculture
Pullman 99163

west virginia
Cooperative Extension Service
West Virginia University
Morgantown 26506

wisconsin
Cooperative Extension Service
University of Wisconsin
432 N. Lake Street
Madison 53706

wyoming
Agricultural Extension Service
University of Wyoming
College of Agriculture
University Station Box 3354
Laramie 82070

where to buy seeds

Burgess Seed & Plant Co.
Galesburg, Mich. 49053

Burnett Brothers, Inc.
92 Chambers Street
New York, N.Y. 10007

W. Atlee Burpee Co.
Warminster, Pa. 18974
Clinton, Iowa 52732
Riverside, Calif. 92502
(write to the office nearest you)

D. V. Burrell Seed Growers Co.
Rocky Ford, Colo. 81067

DeGiorgi Co., Inc.
Seed Growers & Importers
P.O. Box 413
Council Bluffs, Iowa 51501

Farmer Seed & Nursery Co.
Faribault, Minn. 55021

Henry Field Seed and Nursery Co.
Shenandoah, Iowa 51601

Gurney Seed & Nursery Co.
Yankton, S.D. 57078

Joseph Harris Seed Co.
Moreton Farm
Rochester, N.Y. 14624

Charles C. Hart Seed Co.
Wethersfield, Conn. 06109

J. W. Jung Seed Co.
Randolph, Wis. 53956

Earl May Seed & Nursery Co.
Shenandoah, Iowa 51601

Nichols Garden Nursery
1190 N. Pacific Highway
Albany, Ore. 97321

276

L. L. Olds Seed Co.
Madison, Wis. 53701

R. H. Shumway Seedsman
Rockford, Ill. 61101

George W. Park Seed Co.
Greenwood, S.C. 29646

Seedway, Inc.
Hall, N.Y. 14463

Stokes Seeds, Inc.
Box 548
Buffalo, N.Y. 14240

where to buy herb plants

Carroll Gardens
Westminster, Md. 21157

Merry Gardens
Camden, Maine 04843

Cedarbrook Herb Farm
Route 1, Box 1047
Sequim, Wash. 98382

Sunnybrook Farm Nursery
2448 Mayfield Road
Chesterland, Ohio 44026

Herb Cottage
Washington Cathedral
Mount Saint Alban
Washington, D.C. 20016

Taylors Garden
2649 Stingle Avenue
Rosemead, Calif. 91770

Le Jardin du Gourmet
Ramsey, N.J. 07446

Logee's Greenhouses
Danielson, Conn. 06239

Well-Sweep Herb Farm
Mt. Bethel Road
Port Murray, N.J. 07865

books on vegetable gardening

Abraham, George and Katy, *Raise Vegetables Without a Garden.* Countryside Books, Barrington, Ill., 1974.

Ball Blue Book, rev. ed. Ball Corporation, Muncie, Ind., 1974.

Ball Freezer Book. Ball Corporation, Muncie, Ind., 1974.

Better Homes and Gardens Home Canning Cookbook. Meredith Corporation, Des Moines, Iowa, 1973.

Brady, Nyle, *The Nature and Property of Soils.* Macmillan Publishing Co., New York, 1974.

Coulter, Francis, *A Manual of Home Vegetable Gardening.* Dover Publications, New York, 1942 (reprinted 1973).

Courter, Gay, *The Bean Sprout Book.* Simon & Schuster, New York, 1973.

Doty, Walter L., *All About Vegetables.* Chevron Chemical Co., Ortho Division, San Francisco, 1973.

Dragonwagon, Crescent, *Putting Up Stuff for the Cold Time.* Workman Publishing Co., New York, 1973.

Editors of Organic Gardening and Farming Magazine, *Encyclopedia of Organic Gardening.* Rodale Press, Emmaus, Pa., 1974.

Foster, Catharine Osgood, *The Organic Gardener.* Alfred A. Knopf, New York, 1972.

Freezing and Canning Cookbook. Farm Journal and Doubleday & Co., New York, 1973.

Gilmore, Grant and Holly, *Growing Midget Vegetables at Home.* Lancer Books, New York, 1973.

How to Grow Herbs. Lane Magazine and Book Co., Menlo Park, Calif., 1973.

Hunter, Beatrice Trum, *Gardening Without Poisons.* Houghton Mifflin Co., Boston, 1972.

Organic Fertilizers. Rodale Press, Emmaus, Pa., 1973.

Philbrick, Helen and John, *The Bug Book.* Garden Way Publishing, Charlotte, Vt., 1974.

Philbrick, Helen, and Gregg, Richard, *Companion Plants and How to Use Them,* 5th printing. The Devin-Adair Co., Old Greenwich, Conn., 1973.

Robbins, Ann Roe, *25 Vegetables Anyone Can Grow.* Dover Publications, New York, 1942 (reprinted 1974).

Rodale, Robert, *The Basic Book of Organic Gardening.* Ballantine Books, New York, 1971.

Scher, Cary, *The Ten Week Garden.* Something Else Press, Barton, Vt., 1973.

Skelsey, Alice, *Cucumbers in a Flowerpot.* Workman Publishing Co., New York, 1971.

Stout, Ruth, and Clemence, Richard, *No-Work Garden Book.* Rodale Press, Emmaus, Pa., 1973.

Sunset Guide to Organic Gardening. Lane Magazine and Book Co., Menlo Park, Calif., 1972.

Vegetable Gardening. Lane Magazine and Book Co., Menlo Park, Calif., 1973.

Westcott, Cynthia, *The Gardener's Bug Book,* 4th ed. Doubleday & Co., New York, 1973.

index